FROM THE

BRIARPATCH FILE

FROM THE

BRIARPATCH FILE

On Context, Procedure, and American Identity

ALBERT MURRAY

PANTHEON BOOKS

NEW YORK

All rights reserved under International and Pan-American Copyright Conventions. Published in the United States by Pantheon Books, a division of Random House, Inc., New York, and simultaneously in Canada by Random House of Canada Limited, Toronto.

Pantheon Books and colophon are registered trademarks of Random House, Inc.

The following five essays were originally published as book reviews: "The HNIC Who He" appeared as "The Illusive Black Image," in Book-World, *The Chicago Sun Times,* November 19, 1967. · X"Soul Brothers Abroad," *The Chicago Sun Times,* May 19, 1968. · "The Good Old Boys Down Yonder," *The New York Times Book Review,* September 22, 1974. · "The 'Reconstruction' of Robert Penn Warren" appeared as "Asking Questions, Searching Souls," in *The New Leader,* June 21, 1965. · "Louis Armstrong in His Own Words," *The New Republic,* November 22, 1999.

The following two essays were originally published in slightly different form. "The Blue Steel, Rawhide, Patent Leather Implications of Fairy Tales" in *The Georgia Review.* · "An All-Purpose, All-American Literary Intellectual" in *Callaloo.*

Library of Congress Cataloging-in-Publication Data

Murray, Albert.
    From the briarpatch file : on context, procedure, and American identity / Albert Murray.
    ISBN 0-375-42142-4
    1. United States—Intellectual life—20th century. 2. United States—Social conditions—1945–. 3. Arts, American—20th century. 4. African Americans—Intellectual life. 5. African American arts. 6. Murray, Albert. 7. Murray, Albert—Political and social views. I. Title.

E169.12 .M88 2001   306'.0973—dc21   2001031402

www.pantheonbooks.com

Book design by Cassandra J. Pappas

Printed in the United States of America
FIRST EDITION
9 8 7 6 5 4 3 2 1

TO MOZELLE AND MICHELE

Contents

PART I | THE BRIARPATCH

ONE | Antagonistic Cooperation in Alabama

I n the remarks I made on April 16, 1988, at the University of Alabama in Tuscaloosa, where I was a participant in a symposium on "The American South: Distinctiveness and Its Limitations," I began by stating that as a writer of fiction which I hoped would be read as serious literary statement of universal appeal above all else, my primary concern was not with recording, reporting, or documenting sociopolitical data as such about the South.

But then I went on to point out that the universally appealing in art, which is to say aesthetic statement, is always achieved through the extension, elaboration, and refinement of the local details and idiomatic particulars that impinge most intimately on one's everyday existence. So the point was not that I was not at all concerned with writing about the South, but rather that I have always been more interested in ultimate metaphors about the South than in social science surveys about it. Because whereas sociopolitical reports in effect give circumstances which amount to predicament all of the advantages over incentive and ambition, the metaphor may be employed as a pragmatic device that functions as our most basic equipment for living, by which of course I mean self-fulfillment.

The metaphor represents how we *feel* about whatever facts and figures are used to describe or define the concrete circumstances of our existence wherever we are. And how we *feel* adds up to our *outlook* or *horizon of aspiration,* which is the source of our incentive or lack of incentive.

In brief, how I felt about the socioeconomic and political circumstances in the Alabama in which I grew up during the 1920s and the 1930s added up to me thinking of myself as having to be as the ever nimble and ever resourceful mythological Alabama jackrabbit in the no less actual than mythological Alabama briarpatch. Thus I have never thought of myself as a victim or a villain. I was always, *but always,* the fairy tale hero who would marry the fairy tale princess.

All of which is also why I've written so much about the blues (and about jazz, which is the fully orchestrated blues statement). To me, blues music has never been the misery music that the ever so benevolent social-science-survey-oriented do-gooders and uplifters of the downtrodden seem to think it is. To me it has always been good-time music, music that inspires you to stomp away low-down blue feelings and stomp in an atmosphere of earthy well-being and affirmation and celebration of the sheer fact of existence.

Yes, the ever so blue lyrics are indeed about problems, troubles, disappointment, defeat, loss, and unhappiness. But the music, with its locomotive beat and onomatopoeia, not only counterstates and counteracts the complaint that life itself is such a low-down dirty shame, it also goes on to transform the atmosphere (of the juke joint, honky-tonk, or even the rent party) from that of a purification ritual to a fertility ritual! A juke joint, honky-tonk, or any blues dive is a good-time place, and I've never seen, heard, or heard of a blues musician who was not primarily interested in making the good times roll.

Anyway, to me blues music is an aesthetic device of confrontation and improvisation, an existential device or vehicle for coping with the ever-changing fortunes of human existence, in a word entropy, the tendency of everything to become formless. Which is also to say that such music is a device for confronting and acknowledging the harsh fact that the human situation *(the human situation as such)* is always awesome and all too often awful. The blues lyric never lets you forget that.

And yet the blues statement is neither a matter of commiseration nor of protestation as such. According to Kenneth Burke's book *Attitudes Toward History,* aesthetic statement falls into one or the other of two rhetorical frames of reference. On the one hand, there is a frame of *rejection* within which the basic statement is that life should not be a matter of tribulation. Hence the plaint, the complaint, the protestation, the grotesque, the burlesque, the satire, the caricature, the elegy, and so on. But on the other hand there is the frame of *acceptance* of the obvious fact that life is always a struggle against destructive forces and elements whether seen or unseen. Thus the aesthetic statement takes the form of the ode, the hymn of praise, the epic, the tragedy (of noble defeat), the comedy (of insightful resolution), the melodrama (of resolution through effective engineering); and then there is farce, which is where I place the blues and jazz because such music presents life as a matter of perpetual readjustment and improvisation.

Such is the context within which I place my blues-derived literary statement. When Scooter, the protagonist of *Train Whistle Guitar*, *The Spyglass Tree*, and *The Seven League Boots*, says "My name is Jack the Rabbit because I was bred and born and brought up in the briarpatch," he is speaking in terms of the idiomatic particulars of a brown-skin boy from Alabama, but his actions should add up to the anecdotes that represent the basic ancestral American outlook on what life is all about.

As a frame of acceptance the blues as literary statement also functions in terms of the dynamics of *antagonistic cooperation*! In a blues composition or anecdote, a key structural device is the *break*, a cessation of the established rhythm and temp which jazz musicians regard and respond to not as a detrimental or trauma-inducing disruption not unlike the abrupt intrusion of the villain or some other personification of disaster, but rather as an opportunity to exercise their personal best.

What makes the Alabama jackrabbit so nimble, so resilient, so elegantly resourceful? The briarpatch!

TWO | Context and Definition

At Mobile County Training School on the outskirts of Mobile, Alabama, where I was a high school junior in the spring of 1934, you had to compose, memorize, and deliver an essay in the annual juniors' oratorical contest, a major event of the commencement season, of greater importance and only slightly less popular than the annual junior-senior prom. It was an occasion when next year's seniors not only showed their promise but also began their competition for college scholarship grants, without which during those stark days of the Depression many of the most promising among us would not have been able to go to college.

It was while collecting materials in preparation for my oration that I came across a poem by one Langston Hughes. It was in an anthology of writings from the so-called Harlem

Originally written upon receiving the Langston Hughes Medal at City College, New York, in 1997, pages 7–9 were expanded to the present statement in response to receiving the Clarence Cason Medal for Distinguished Nonfiction Writing at the University of Alabama in 2001.

Renaissance entitled *The New Negro,* edited by Alain Locke. The poem was called "Youth," and not only did I memorize it and use it as the outchorus for my statement, I also appropriated the title of Alain Locke's anthology as the theme and title of my presentation.

Well, Langston's poem didn't win the juniors' oratorical contest for me. But along with Locke's theme it did lead the sponsors to choose me as the lead-off speaker, which meant that faculty support for my college scholarship grant status was already very strong indeed.

I can't say that Langston Hughes or anybody else from the so-called Harlem Renaissance as such inspired me to be a writer. Once I got to college and became involved with literature as existential equipment for living rather than as academic exercises and ceremonial-recitation fluff stuff, nothing in *The New Negro* struck me as being in the same league as such world-class twentieth-century writers as James Joyce, Thomas Mann, Marcel Proust, André Malraux, Ernest Hemingway, William Faulkner, T. S. Eliot, W. B. Yeats, and Ezra Pound, among others. Which is to say there was nothing from my idiomatic American context in literature that was comparable to what Jack Johnson, Joe Gans, Sam Langford, and the up-and-coming young Joe Louis represented as world-class prizefighters, or Eddie Tolan, Ralph Metcalfe, and Jesse Owens as Olympic-class track stars; nor was there any question in my mind that segregation kept Satchel Paige and Josh Gibson from being unsurpassed in the world of baseball. And that Louis Armstrong and Duke Ellington represented the very best that America had to offer in music went without saying. In other words, segregation was no excuse.

The point here is that, taking my clue from the world-class aesthetic, sophistication, and profundity of Armstrong,

Jelly Roll Morton, Ellington, Basie, Lester Young, Dizzy Gillespie, Charlie Parker, and other definitive masters of what I refer to as the blues idiom (the ultimate extension, elaboration, and refinement of which is jazz), I decided that I would try to produce a literary equivalent of the world-class fine art music that they had processed from the idiomatic particulars of my most immediate and intimate American context.

You, of course, know that the ambition to produce world-class literature involves the matter of processing or stylizing idiomatic folk and pop particulars, which is to say extending, elaborating, and refining folk and pop material up to the level of fine art. Thus the jazz musicians that I am forever referring to were indispensable to me as an apprentice writer because what they did was develop the technique and sophistication necessary to transform folk and pop music into aesthetic statement that qualified as fine art and that has had the universal appeal, impact, profundity, and endurance of fine art.

As for my personal existential and literary point of view, the main thing is not some putative subtext that some academics seek out as if the writer has either hidden it or really doesn't know that it is there. The indispensable thing is the rhetorical context, the basic frame of reference that conditions the nature of the aesthetic statement that one's stylization of actuality adds up to.

My basic working assumption is that all literary statements fall into one or the other of two categories or frames of reference that represent two opposite attitudes toward experience or the circumstances of human existence: (1) the frame of acceptance or (2) the frame of rejection. These attitudes condition literary responses.

In other words, you can either accept the harsh facts of

life and do what you can to counteract or ameliorate them, such as what has been done to counteract bad weather. Or you can cry and shiver and feel sorry for yourself. Thus, on the one hand you have the literary image-statement of the questing and conquesting storybook hero who is still a hero and merits celebration even when he fails. Hence the epic, tragedy, comedy, melodrama, and farce. Whereas on the other hand what you have is the lamenting, protesting, perpetually pissed-off rebel who *rejects* the all too obvious fact that life is not always fair, weatherwise or otherwise, and who sees himself not as a potential self-made hero but as a victim of foul play!

All of my books are about the basis and possibilities of heroic action that are endemic to life in the United States in our time. That is why the name of my storybook hero in *Train Whistle Guitar, The Spyglass Tree,* and *The Seven League Boots* is Scooter and why he refers to himself as Jack the Rabbit and says that he was bred, born, and raised in the - briarpatch and realizes that his possibilities of survival, not to mention achievement, are predicated on his perpetual nimbleness, which means that he must always be ready to swing as if he were a competent jazz musician in the ever unpredictable circumstances of a jam session and also always be ready to riff or improvise on the break.

In the early-twentieth-century Viennese mythology of Sigmund Freud and others, the break may well have been regarded as a sudden disruption in the established cadence, the effect of which was very likely to be shocking, traumatic, and even disabling. In American legend, however, although the break is a matter of jeopardy, it is also regarded as a matter of opportunity. In the blues idiom it is also the moment of truth and of proof!

And now, one more bit of signifying about Scooter as Brer Rabbit in the complexities of the contemporary American briarpatch. The one thing that faked Brer Rabbit out was a phony image of his people! What I see when I look at social science surveys and profiles of "my people" (which is to say, my idiomatic American relatives) is a bunch of social science fiction tar babies!

Down-home boy that I am, I have never been so unhip, so unbelievably square, as to mistake a tar baby for the me I think I should be, certainly not because some social science head-counting racial one-upman decides that a tar baby stands for all rabbits.

My rabbit, it turns out, is not literally the same as the one that old Uncle Remus used to tell the little bright-eyed boy over in Georgia about. My rabbit is the Alabama jackrabbit version of the one that Duke Ellington had in mind when he orchestrated the concerto for tenor saxophone entitled Cotton Tail.

WHEN I GRADUATED from Tuskegee in 1939, it was as if the soundtrack of the world of adult adventure that I was finally entering on my own authority was Count Basie's "Doggin' Around," a Kansas City 4/4 stomp number that may well have been a variation on an earlier shout tune entitled "Messin' Around" ("All over Town!") recorded by Trixie Smith and Freddie Keppard back in the 1920s. What was so profoundly impressive to me about this particular version of it was the elegant ease of each solo instrumentalist, who not only coped with the pressure of the band's up-tempo environment but also established and maintained his own distinctive individuality at the same time. Every time I remember the challenges of the uncertainties I faced that summer after college as I waited to find out what my first job offer was going to be, I also remember that old ten-inch, 72-rpm recording on the other side of which was a very melancholy instrumental torch tune entitled "Blue and Sentimental." I wondered if I would ever be able to respond to the pressures and requirements of the twentieth-century world at large as if dancing to Count Basie's "Doggin' Around."

That was in 1939. Then in 1940 came Duke Ellington's "Cotton Tail." I had been personalizing Ellington's music since 1927 when I was eleven years old, and my most intimate playmate and I realized that we could do our notorious, sporty limp walk to Ellington's "Birmingham Breakdown" with the same sneaky cuteness with which we were already doing it to old Jellyroll Morton's "Kansas City Stomp."

Between elementary school and college there were Ellington's "Rockin' in Rhythm," "It Don't Mean a Thing if It Ain't Got That Swing," "Daybreak Express," and "Harlem Speaks." And among those from that next four years that have meant most to me were "Diminuendo and Crescendo in Blue," "Tootin' Through the Roof," "Chatterbox," "Braggin' in Brass," "Boy Meets Horn," and "Ridin' on a Blue Note."

Count Basie's "Doggin' Around" provided me with the soundtrack that I needed for 1939. But it was Ellington's "Cotton Tail" that was a specific source for the metaphor of the nimble-or-nothing Alabama jackrabbit in the briar-patch, evoking tell-me-tale times around the fireplace in that shotgun-style quarters house on the outskirts of Mobile down off the Gulf Coast that was to become the idiomatic basis for my literary approach to American character, procedure, and heroic achievement.

In her *American Humor: A Study of the National Character,* Constance Rourke, a number of whose essays on the same subject were published posthumously as *The Roots of American Culture,* wrote about the ingenious Yankee, the adventurous frontiersman, and the adaptable Negro as a definitive mythic trio that provided *emblems for a pioneer people who require resilience as a prime trait,* resilience that is geared to spontaneous exploration, experimentation, inventiveness, and perpetual readjustment.

The challenge for me, as an apprentice of literature as a fine art, has been how to process local and regional folk or peasant (including illiterate) material beyond the limitations of the provincial and beyond the platitudes of pop fare and achieve the universal appeal and status of fine art. This requires the most reliable insight into the nature of human nature, the most basic appreciation of the complexity of our national imperatives, and the most refined mastery of the means of literary composition available.

What the valid, reliable, and comprehensive literary image should add up to is that which Kenneth Burke in *Attitudes Toward History* called the representative anecdote, a symbolic representation of survival and achievement. So far, what I've been able to do with the image of the Alabama jackrabbit in the briarpatch is to be found in *Train Whistle Guitar, The Spyglass Tree,* and *The Seven League Boots,* which have no less to do with the rituals underlying the adventures of Tom Sawyer and Huckleberry Finn, for instance, than with "Doggin' Around," "Cotton Tail," or "C-Jam Blues." In fact, Scooter may even be thought of as Huck Finn's friend Jim's great-grandson.

THREE | Academic Lead Sheet

W hat I have prepared for this extremely important occasion is not a formal address, but rather an outline for some not quite solemn but altogether ceremonial remarks, to which I hope you will respond as if to such ever so avuncular advice as comes from the fire circle of the elders of your tribe, among whom I must say I am more than somewhat astonished to find myself.

Or if you prefer a somewhat less anthropological and more idiomatic analogy, I would be no less pleased to have you respond as your grandparents did to what they heard and overheard from the grownups around the firesides in the old down-home cabins of yesteryear during those evenings when so much hard-bought wisdom was imparted along with the very stuff of such ambition as brings us all here today.

This essay is based on an address given on January 20, 1978, at the Howard University Honors Convocation.

And, to be sure, there is always all of that ever so off-hand signifying that I myself was so privileged to grow up hearing and overhearing in the barbershops and on the general merchandise store stoop benches during the days of my coming of age on the outskirts of Mobile, Alabama. Such barbershops and storefront benches as were the hangouts of such legendary uncles as Uncle Bud, Uncle Doc, Uncle Ned, and Uncle Remus, among others.

In other words, the brief notes that I have jotted down for this talk are not an outline for formal pontification but are somewhat like a minimal lead sheet for a bit of riff style signifying such as may be associated with what comes from the piano in a jazz performance. Not such consummate statements as come from such fabulous keyboard soloists as, say, Art Tatum, Teddy Wilson, Earl Hines, and Bud Powell, to be sure, but rather from such suggestive vamping and comping as were used by such peerless keyboard masters as Duke Ellington and Count Basie to provide the contexts within which individual sidemen in their orchestras not only established but also developed their individual identities.

Nor, by the way, did even such super soloists as Johnny Hodges, Ben Webster, Cootie Williams, Lester Young, Dicky Wells, and Harry Edison misconstrue Ellington's and Basie's background setups as launching pads for ego trips. On the contrary, each of their most distinctive individual solos represented an indispensable dimension of the overall ensemble statement.

In other words, I come before you on this occasion as a sort of academic equivalent to a vamping and comping piano player in what amounts to an intellectual jam session in which your responses are no less real for not being heard.

Indeed I hope that the solos, ensembles, arrangements, and orchestrations that my contextual vamps, comp chords, and progressions suggest will speak or sing or swing louder than any actual vocal or instrumental voicings ever can.

End of vamp. First chorus: This is the occasion on which the school officials celebrate the good students, the successful students. We are assembled here today to acknowledge and celebrate pupils whom special members of the faculty have selected as those whose academic performance qualifies them to be candidates to take on the indispensable responsibilities of being the elite of the generation now coming of age. Elite. Yes, elite. And again elite. Don't allow yourselves to be faked out by epithets. If elitism bothers you, substitute the word specialist and get on with the mission.

Can any group, based on whatever distinction, even survive, let alone develop and fulfill itself (to say nothing of transcending itself), without the benefit of its own elite corps of highly competent and dedicated intellectual, professional, and technical specialists? Obviously such an elite was what W. E. B. Du Bois had in mind when he advocated the development of what he called the Talented Tenth. Nor were Booker T. Washington's agricultural, technical, and normal school missionaries expected to add up to anything less than an even larger elite corps that was to include the big moneymakers.

The function of the elite is to provide the rest of society with equipment for living which is commensurate with the complexity and possibilities of the time in which they live. You have to be specialists in order to do that. And we hope that at least some of you are also geniuses. And you know something? If all the students of this institution were assembled here because they have grade point averages that qualify them as outstanding achievers, that would not be enough.

Indeed if all Americans were fully educated, technologically proficient, and productive, mankind in the world at large would still be in trouble. Perhaps it would be somewhat better off, to be sure, but the need for a continuous input of dedicated special achievers would be no less urgent.

And yet there are those who give a very strong impression that dropouts and self-reformed or cult-redeemed excons who opt for the authority and responsibility of the elite can contend successfully with outstanding graduates from such world-class centers of precision and comprehensiveness as Heidelberg, Oxford, Cambridge, the Sorbonne, Harvard, Yale, Princeton, MIT, Caltech, and so on.

But certainly nobody on this campus is gong to fall for such an unhip line of jive. Certainly everybody in this academic gathering knows enough about what "street smarts" is about—to know that street hip is not about such mathematical calculations as add up to space technology or computer science. Nor does the jive lingo of the street-corner hangout add up to the linguistic prerequisite to understanding anthropology, archaeology, or even the plain old ancient, medieval, and modern history and geopolitics underlying foreign policy. And so forth and so on, you get the point.

That was about leadership. But what kind of leadership? The big thing these days seems to be revolutionary leadership. So a quick segue to another matter that our most promising students should be alert to. Everywhere you go these days you find a significant number of students who seem to want to be regarded as revolutionary above everything else. But many confuse revolution with rebellion. Which is sometimes only a matter of rejecting or even destroying established procedures and institutions. But the primary concern of revolution is not destruction but the creation of better procedures and institutions. All too often being a rebel means only that you're against something. Whereas being a revolutionary should mean that you are *against* something because you are *for* something better. Indeed, primarily because you're for something better.

But the special fireside-and-barbershop-derived piano riff on revolutionary leadership that I wish to suggest is that, in contrast to many of the news media and storybook revolutionary heroes who often began with the problem of rejecting the conventional values of their forebears, the good American student from our ethnic and idiomatic background has only to try to prepare to become the living answer to the old folks' prayers.

The rebellion part, as rugged as it may get to be from time to time, is only incidental. It is the revolutionary change that counts. And all we have to do in order to contribute our part to achieving that is what our American, repeat American, grandparents and great-grandparents wanted their heirs to do. Everybody on this campus is the descendant of forebears who hoped and prayed that you would be outstanding students. What could be more subversive in the United States! And yet all that even the most activist of our antebellum ancestors wanted was the fulfillment of the promise inherent in the Constitution of the United States of America.

Which brings us back to the function of the elite. My concern here is not with the certified professions, the doctors, lawyers, scientists, engineers, and so on. My immediate concern is with the intellectuals and the artists. For it is they who provide the context for the so-called spokesmen and civic leaders (self- or otherwise elected). The function of the artist is to create images or the musical equivalents thereof that are commensurate with the complexities and the possibilities of life in our time. Whereas the intellectual or so-called thinking person has a responsibility to formulate questions, issues, and definitions that adequately reflect the problems of the times and thus form a basis that adequate specialized technicians can build on.

So our intellectuals must try to be sure that they are defining problems and issues in the most comprehensive terms. The intellectual's very first step should represent an effort to approach life in universal terms. Sentimental provincialism is out! Your ambition should be to become as cosmopolitan as possible. Now, you reach the universal or the cosmopolitan through the particular. So obviously you do not have to abandon your idiomatic roots. Indeed the more you dig down into yourself and deal with your personal problems against the richest possible background (and thus in the broadest context), the more universal the implications of your most casual personal gesture is likely to become.

I submit that as a responsible intellectual you proceed in terms of extension (as well as elaboration and refinement) and also counterstatement. You extend, elaborate, and refine that which you test and judge to be adequate, the objective being to give it its greatest precision and effectiveness. On the other hand, you counterstate that which you judge to be inadequate, unproductive, or counterproductive or which violates your sense of life in some way. Here, incidentally, is where the element of protest comes in.

You reject that which is unproductive or counterproductive. But you don't reduce everything to rejection and rebellion, because the whole idea of life, which is to say the process of living or continuing to exist, is affirmation. The whole idea of education is to find the terms and meanings that make fruitful continuity possible.

Protest is something that you must always be extremely careful about, because it can degenerate so easily into the self-righteousness of those who regard themselves as victims rather than people of potential and thus become more emotional than insightful and corrective. Militant rhetoric is not enough. And besides, it doesn't require the high grade point average that the truly qualified leader must earn. What with the news media being as they are these days, any street-corner jive artist can bring it off.

So where do I myself as a writer fit into all of this? Well, speaking of the need for the most comprehensive frame of reference that a literary intellectual and would-be pragmatic image-maker might suggest for coming to terms with the imperatives of the human proposition in a contemporary world, the most impressive device I've come across so far is very idiomatic indeed. It is the blues idiom, which I have come to regard as being the basic part of the existential equipment that we Americans inherited from our captive ancestors.

Many people seem to think that all the slaves left us was a legacy of misery. I don't agree. They also endowed us with an attitude toward life that the blues idiom embodies. Which is in essence a disposition of affirmation of continuity in the face of adversity. The basic dynamics of the blues idiom are predicated upon confrontation or acknowledgment of the harsh facts of life. The fact that not only is one's personal plight sometimes pretty awful and unpromising, but also that life itself often looks like a low-down dirty shame that shouldn't happen to any creature imaginable. The blues require you to confront chaos as a fact of life and improvise on the exigencies of the situation, however dire, on the opportunities or the options that are also always there.

I've come to believe that the blues idiom provides the basis for a more comprehensive context for literary statement than any of the masterpieces in the anthology of world literature. As I have pointed out in my book *The Hero and the Blues,* it is a context which enables one to deal with the tragic, comic, melodramatic, and farcical dimensions of existence simultaneously. In the fully orchestrated blues statement, even as the tragic tale of woe (and blues lyrics are almost always negative) is being spieled by the soloist, it is being counterstated by the instruments—and not just with determination, but sometimes with bawdiness, sometimes insouciance, sometimes just devilishly, sometimes with nonsense or just plain old foolishness, but also always with a lot of elegance.

Because it turns out that a definitive characteristic of the descendants of American slaves is an orientation to elegance, the disposition (in the face of all of the misery and uncertainty in the universe) to refine all of human action in a direction of dance-beat elegance. I submit that there is nothing that anybody in the world has ever done that is more civilized or sophisticated than to dance elegantly, which is to state with your total physical being an affirmative attitude toward the sheer fact of existence. Talking about getting with it. Swinging the blues is something *else!*

So now for an outchorus of sorts. It seems to me that

the legacy that I refer to as the blues idiom offers many crucial opportunities for good students who would really deal with the problems not only of one special group of people in contemporary America but of mankind in the world at large. One little example: you all know about that big concept of disjuncture as being trauma-producing and disintegrating that is so basic to contemporary psychology and psychiatry (or what I call Viennese mythology)! Well, in the blues idiom no less is made of the necessity to establish a form, a rhythm, a cadence, and a meaningful direction, the absence of which makes for that discombobulation that is precisely the effect also known as being blue or having the blues.

But in a blues performance there is also a very deliberate and indispensable disjuncture which, however, is not regarded as a crisis. It is called a break, and it has a double meaning. It is a disruption but it is also an opportunity. It is a moment of high jeopardy to be sure. But it is at the very same time a moment of truth, the moment in which your response defines your personal quality and identity.

The break is the very thing that every American worthy of the name is supposed to make preparations to take advantage of. And what that requires is precisely the same orientation to such ongoing improvisation as sustained the early American explorers, pioneers, frontiersmen, and homesteaders. In a word, perpetual creativity!

Or to put it another way, a musical break peculiar to the blues is a stylization or aesthetic statement that represents a basic American attitude toward experience or outlook on life. To this end it not only conditions one to regard disjuncture as a normal expectation but also should develop the resilience that facilitates improvisation. Incidentally, the disposition and proficiency required of the improvising blues musician and that required for scientific experimentation is not as different as many people might think.

There is a problem of disjuncture and there is also the problem of the rootlessness that is such an obvious and widespread result of twentieth-century technological innovations. Homesteads, for example, do not mean what they used to mean. Bulldozers wipe them out in no time at all. Homesteads, hometowns, and many other traditional landmarks as well.

As rootless as the pioneers or even the captive Africans were, contemporary mankind in the world at large may well be in a predicament that is basically worse. Naming all of your ethnic ancestors all the way back to Ham or even Adam and Eve is not likely to do very much to help you cope with contemporary instability nearly so well as a blues-conditioned disposition to remain perpetually resilient and alert to the ongoing need for improvisation.

The ancestors that are likely to be most useful to students in our time are those to whom, regardless of their ethnicity, honor students are required to relate themselves in the established courses in the great universities. I submit that the greatest challenge to the good student of our time is to learn as much as you can from the documented experiential data that has come down to us through the ages and then continue to look for something better.

PART II | THE CREATIVE PROCESS

ONE | Art As Such

The following remarks are based on the assumption that there is no such thing as *applied* art. Art does what it does on its own terms or it is not art. Art should not be confused with propaganda, advertisement, ideology, or hype of any kind. These remarks are concerned with the primordial nature and function of aesthetic endeavor, and thus they are about what any work of art can reasonably be expected to represent.

Nor should this be confused with the old so-called ivory tower notion of art for art's sake. On the contrary, the primary emphasis here is on art, which is to say aesthetic statement, as fundamental equipment for existence on human terms. The primary concern of art is not with beauty per se, as many people seem to think, but with the quality of human consciousness.

Keynote address at the Alabama State Council on the Arts Statewide Arts Conference at Perdido Beach, February 17, 1994.

Thus these remarks are geared to a very pragmatic conception and approach to art. So are all of the books that I have published as a student of cultural dynamics and as an apprentice of the creative process. And so are the two works in progress. Naturally I hope that what follows will add up to a useful reiteration of essential definitions and the indispensable objectives that are crucial to all decisions about artistic undertakings of any kind.

I also hope you will agree that a conference of artists, arts administrators, board members of arts organizations, educators, public officials, and other interested people is a most appropriate audience for the review and reiteration I have in mind. After all, who, for instance, could possibly be more disturbed by the threat that the pressure to be politically correct represents to the ambitions of serious artists who accept the challenge that the great world classics embody?

Nor, by the way, does it help matters in the least that the pressure and restrictions of political correctness are being exerted in the guise of well-intentioned permissiveness in the interests of what our current crop of do-gooders think of as the empowerment of the downtrodden. Why should anybody's efforts to equate inaccuracy and mediocrity with excellence be indulged?

I submit that such questions are directly related to the policies, proposals, requests, and programs that councils on the arts have to consider every day. In any case, I hope you will agree that a review of fundamental definitions and assumptions is always useful, even to master craftsmen.

Not that I really expect to do justice to the issue in the format of an after-dinner talk. After all, I usually deal with such matters in semester-length university seminars. But

you can always supplement what I am saying here by reading *The Hero and the Blues,* which is about literature, and
Stomping the Blues, which is about music, and also *The Omni-
Americans,* which is about the inadequacy of images based
on social science theory and categories rather than precise
insight and hard-earned wisdom.

In any case, point one: Art as such is a means by which
the raw materials of human experience are processed into
aesthetic statement. In this instance, to process is to stylize.
So the work of art is stylization become statement, *aesthetic
statement.* That is the objective of the creative process. And
one assumes that it is also the sole objective of all grants
from councils on the arts, since grants for other kinds of
statements are funded by other councils and agencies.

What a work of art represents, which is to say re-*presents,*
presents again, reenacts, reproduces, recalls, is not actuality
per se, no matter how vivid the evocation of concrete detail,
but rather how the artist feels about something. Indeed literal facts and figures are only incidental to a work of art.
After all, given adequate stylization, fantasy and deliberate
distortion will work just as well. Let us not forget that fables
and fairy tales are as believable as naturalistic novels, precisely documented movies, and news-oriented television.

According to Susanne K. Langer, what art as such really
records is the life of human feeling, how it feels to be a
human being in this or that situation. Hence the feeling
tones represented by tragedy, melodrama, and farce. And
Kenneth Burke suggests that art is really a stylization of a
basic attitude toward human existence. Hence expressive
forms that condition people to accept the necessity for persistent struggle, on the one hand, and forms on the other
hand that lament and protest human predicament. Inciden-

tally, those who accept the necessity for struggle are also given to forms for the celebration of courage before danger, gallantry in defeat, and also forms for rejoicing in victory.

Another definition. Works of art are the product of an elegant extension, elaboration, and refinement of rituals that reenact the basic (and thus definitive) survival technology of people in a given time, place, and circumstance. Which is why the main concern of art is the quality of human consciousness. Thus, it is also fundamental existential equipment in that it not only provides emblems of a basic attitude toward experience but also conditions and disposes people to behave in accordance with a given lifestyle (or survival technology!).

Which brings us to a brief natural history of aesthetic statement as such. First there is ritual, the ceremonial reenactment of the basic survival technology. Rituals enable anthropologists to define the basic occupations and security measures and thus also the characteristic orientation, mindset, or *preoccupations* of any given social configuration, whether tribal, regional, or national. Primal rituals include ceremonial reenactments of hunting, fishing, sowing, tilling, and harvesting, and warfare as well as continuity through purification and fertility.

Ritual reenactment supervised by a priesthood becomes religion, which also generates its own specific internal ceremonies of devotion and propitiation, which I mention only in passing along with magic, which is another kind of ceremonial reenactment.

In addition to religion and magic there is also the no less aboriginal matter of *playful* reenactment, which we refer to as recreation, and which indeed is literally a matter of re-creation, re-presentation, and re-producing. Thus the essential character or disposition of a nation as well as a tribe may be discerned in its games and toys.

But the key point of this brief natural history is that it is from the playful reenactment of primal ritual that art as such is most directly derived. I submit that not to understand this is to miss the very basis of aesthetic evaluation and critical judgment.

As you know, some play activities are restricted by rules and regulations, and some are also supervised by umpires and referees and judges, and some are not. But you also know, even the most closed codified play activity permits personal options from which not only individual expression but also individual improvisation, stylization, and elegance emerge. And it is the extension, elaboration, and refinement of such option-taking that adds up to the aesthetic statement that is a work of art. Which is to say, a product of elegant artifice.

A few more words about the role of play in the creative process. There are, according to Roger Caillois in *Man, Play, and Games,* four categories of play activity and two directions of playful effort. The categories are competition, chance, make-believe, and vertigo. And playful effort may be just a matter of fooling around, on the one hand, or a matter of gratuitously increasing the difficulty of execution on the other. This aspect of playful reenactment is obviously a key source of the extension, elaboration, and refinement that adds up to works of art.

So now a few words about the relative level of sophistication of technique and sensibility involved in the creative process. What this results in are three levels of achievement: folk art, pop fare, and fine art.

Folk art should not be confused with primitive art,

although some visual arts commentaries refer to it as modern primitive. *To the extent that primitive artifacts are perceived as art rather than as ceremonial fetishes, they are neither folk art nor pop fare but fine art, because they are the handiwork of the most sophisticated skill in the culture of their origin.*

Folk art is the output of the least refined skill and the least precise information and the least subtle sensibility in a culture that is also capable of producing pop fare and fine art. It may be genuine and also deeply moving, but even so it is also likely to have a more limited range of appeal than pop fare or fine art. Which is not to say that it is emotionally less authentic than pop fare. It is, on the contrary, a more honest representation than pop fare, which is, after all, often given to gimmickry, cliché, cheap sentimentality, and downright vulgarity.

Yet the range and skill involved in pop-level stylization are such that it may include elements that are not only crude but also illiterate, along with devices expertly appropriated from the most highly calibrated levels of fine art. A major shortcoming of pop fare is shallowness and the rapidity with which most of it goes out of fashion.

Which brings us to fine art. Being the ultimate extension, elaboration, and refinement of the most representative images, anecdotes, and soundtracks, it may be sometimes less immediately accessible than folk art in its native province or pop fare in the world at large. But is it not precisely the function of courses in art appreciation to make fine art accessible? The very first obligation of critical briefings and reviews is to mediate between the uninitiated audiences, viewers, or readers and the work of art.

The purpose of reviewing these distinctions in degrees of sophistication involved in stylization is to remind you of the role that taste plays in all aesthetic matters. How can you make any truly useful decision about the arts if you are deficient in your perception of nuance or indifferent to propriety? Now, I am very keenly aware of the fact that many of our fellow Americans become somewhat uneasy, if not embarrassingly defensive, at the mere mention of aesthetic taste.

But taste in the arts is pretty much the same as it is in the kitchen and the dining room. It is the sense of the optimum proportion and processing of the ingredients required by a given recipe. In the arts taste begins with your sensitivity to the nuances of a given process of stylization being such that you would not confuse folk art, pop fare, and fine art. Each has its place. But it is fine art from which come the masterpieces that add up to the classic examples that make up the universal anthology, the worldwide repertory, the museum without walls that underlies our most comprehensive conception of human potential or indeed the human proposition.

If any of this sounds the least bit elitist to any of you, ask yourself if you really prefer anything but the most competent craftsmen, doctors, dentists, lawyers, teachers, or even servants, etc. Most people obviously prefer all-star quality over mediocrity in sports. Why not in the arts?

TWO | Riffing at Mrs. Jack's Place

E ye of the beholder. Eye of the beholder. Eye of the beholder, indeed. And never forget that point of view is synonymous with angle of vision, which also involves depth of field and sharpness of focus.

And as Mrs. Isabella Stewart Gardner obviously assumed, so is perception geared to apperception, that process of understanding and appreciation through which the newly observed qualities of an object are related to past experience. For certainly she was concerned with the background of the beholder: what the observer brings to the object on view, that which makes for the context of the onlooker's interaction with it.

Incidentally, there is convincing evidence that Mrs. Gardner was concerned not only with what her collection could add to the background that her fellow Americans would bring to the certified masterworks of Europe, she was also providing levels of aesthetic excellence by which Americans could measure their own efforts to create fine art from the raw materials of their native environment.

In other words, for all the intimidation it may have evoked from many upper-class, middle-class, and lower-class Bostonians alike, this Venetian palace was not built to insulate an ever so effete Mrs. Gardner from the crude actualities of everyday life in the still ever so frontierlike ruggedness of the United States at the turn of the century. For certainly hard-bargaining, hands-on Mrs. Jack Gardner was too hip not to know that the now magnificent Italians of the now hallowed Renaissance were themselves products of the extension, elaboration, and refinement of the barbarians of Europe of the Dark and Middle Ages.

Which is not to imply that she herself was as keenly, profoundly, and comprehensively aware of the dynamics of the evolution of a national character and its stylization in the fine arts as Constance Rourke (author of *American Humor: A Study of the National Character,* 1931) was to become within less that a decade of Mrs. Gardner's demise. But it most certainly is meant to insist that she was a very fundamental part of the natural history suggested by Constance Rourke, as well as John A. Kouwenhoven's notion of the effects of the interaction of imported learned traditions or practices with vernacular or homespun methods in the context of the pragmatic improvisation required of a pioneer people such as Americans still are.

Van Wyck Brooks pointed out that for all her discriminating taste and her unimpeachable collection, Mrs. Jack saw "Giogione's finest points as she saw the virtues of Whistler and Sargent who blazed like meteors over the world of fashion. But she did not see the Yankee Giogiones," by whom he meant Maurice Prendergast, Winslow Homer, and Albert Ryder. But even so, Fenway Court, like the Boston Museum of Fine Arts, the Metropolitan Museum of Art in New York, and countless others, has always been and continues to be an indispensable element in the development of the high level of aesthetic sensibility that American artists have achieved in the twentieth century.

Because for all its palatial walls of thoroughly convincing Old World patina on which hang some of the finest European art in the Western Hemisphere, Mrs. Jack's Eyetalian Palace also functions as a part of what has been called the museum without walls, what in effect is an imaginary universal museum that all the art in the world adds up to, a sort of visual equivalent of a *bibliothèque pléiade,* a worldwide anthology of literature. The creative impulse, after all, as André Malraux has pointed out, is at least as much a response to other aesthetic statements as it is to raw experience. In other words, art derives from other art.

Along with the obvious implications of all this for the specialist in the arts, there is also the no less obvious fact that twentieth-century innovations in and refinements of communication and transportation facilities have made even the most sedentary Americans nothing less than citizens of the world at large in spite of themselves. Indeed, the world at large impinges on the sensibilities of average Americans as it does on no other general populace elsewhere on the contemporary globe. Nor should the fact that this impingement includes an ever-increasing influx of immigrants from pretty nearly everywhere be overlooked.

Because of all of this, it is not only possible but also obviously necessary for a contemporary American's conception of aesthetic statement to be more and more comprehensive, even more and certainly no less comprehensive than that of the most sophisticated elite of the British and French empires in their heyday. The characterization of "heiress of all the ages" that Henry James applied to the heroine of *Daisy Miller,* Milly Theale of *The Wings of the Dove,* and Maggie Verver of *The Golden Bowl* not only applied to his friend Mrs. Isabella Stewart Gardner as well but to all contemporary Americans.

And now for a few hard-driving choruses about the nature and function of aesthetic statement as such, which after all is what is really under consideration here. For what is artistic creation if not the means by which raw or actual experience is processed, by which is meant stylized, into aesthetic statement? An aesthetic statement which in effect is an *elegant* statement is precisely what all works of art are intended to be. Thus painting and sculpture are visual statements even as literature is verbal statement, and a piece of music is statement made with sound and rhythm, and so on. In any case, art appreciation is a matter of decoding the stylized statement, which is made in the terminology peculiar to the medium in which the artist works.

Also it should be remembered that a statement may be either denotative or connotative. A denotative statement is meant to be taken literally. Its aim is a precise representation of actuality. The ultimate in denotation is scientific terminology. A connotative statement is primarily evocative and may actually be deliberately ambiguous, figuratively, symbolic, ironic, hyperbolic, and so on, in a word poetic.

Furthermore, art, being stylized statement, is of its very nature connotative rather than denotative; hence figures of speech and devices of sound in literary statement and devices of rhythm, melody, harmony, and tone color in music, and so on. In all events, the primary objective of aesthetic statement is not literal documentation as such, but rather the equivalent of the representative anecdote in literature. It is thus a record not of facts as such, but of the emotional response of a given sensibility. It is a stylized statement of an emotional response to an experience which in itself may be either real or imagined. Which is why we look at a visual statement and identify it as a Botticelli, Bellini, or Raphael, or call a literary statement Shakespeare, Goethe, Thomas Mann, James, Joyce, Hemingway, Faulkner, and so on. And a piece of music as Bach, Mozart, Beethoven, Stravinsky, Armstrong, Basie, Ellington, or Charlie Parker.

On the other hand, the more denotative the statement, which is to say the more literal the documentation, the greater the risk that the result will belong to the category of genre rather than becoming a representative anecdote and thus a vehicle for conveying such profound insights into the universal ambiguities and contradictions of the human situation as do totally unrealistic fables and fairy tales. Genre is about what something is like and thus may even be a stylization of the obvious and may actually be intended as a commonplace illustration.

The representative anecdote, on the other hand, is about possible implications and thus may be deliberately ambiguous, which is to say multidimensional, as stylized statements that qualify as fine art always turn out to be.

So now a few words about fine art as such. The process of stylization, or, as André Malraux would say, the creative act, proceeds on one of three levels of technological sophistication. As a result there is folk art, there is popular art fare, and there is fine art, which represent three different levels of extension, elaboration, and refinement of the basic and indeed the definitive rituals of the social or cultural configuration that is its context.

Folk art is a product of the no less serious or humorous,

no less authentic but least informed and crudest aesthetic sensibility of a given social or cultural entity that is capable of producing a more widely appealing popular art that is technically more accomplished and better informed although it may also employ peasant-level naïveté and crudeness along with ever so chic devices consciously derived from fine art. Incidentally, folk art should not be confused with primitive art, as many critics and historians did for many years. For to the extent that the stylization of primitive, aboriginal, or downright primordial artifacts are viewed as art, they are not folk art but fine art because they are the product not of the lowest but rather of the most highly developed skills of stylization produced by the culture of their origin. Indeed fine art is precisely the ultimate extension, elaboration, and refinement of the fundamental rituals underlying the lifestyle survival techniques of the people, whether tribe or nation, by whom it is created.

And now for the outchorus plus a tag.

Much goes to show that the worldwide museum without walls that includes not only Fenway Court and the Boston Museum of Fine Arts across the way but the Metropolitan Museum of New York and the British Museum and the Louvre across the Atlantic, among all the rest; not only museums and galleries but also all of the art books and reproductions available here and elsewhere exist to inspire through the eye of the beholder an ever keener appreciation plus an ongoing demand for the very highest level of fine art.

Which also means multidimensional representative anecdotes, not simply the annals of the activities and incidents of a specific time and place. That would amount to provincialism even if it were the stylization of typical activities of a great metropolis. The great masterworks are about the human proposition as such, the struggle of human consciousness against chaos, the void, entropy. Yes, stylization is yet another way, the more elegant the better, of contending with entropy, of stomping the blues, which is to say, of keeping the blue devils of nada at bay.

THREE

Made in America:

The Achievement of

Duke Ellington

On the eve of the New York premiere of his Symphony no. 9 in E Minor, *From the New World*, in 1893, Anton Dvořák stated in an interview that he was "now satisfied that the future music of this country must be founded upon what are called the Negro melodies. They must be the real foundation of any serious and original school of composition to be developed in the United States."

Dvořák had been brought over to New York from Bohemia in 1892 by one Mrs. Jeannette Thurber, the wife of a wealthy New York grocer, to help establish a national conservatory of music of America, the objective of which was to develop American composers who would follow the example of what Dvořák had done with the Slavonic folk materials of Bohemia and create music from indigenous

American sources that would qualify as fine art worthy of being performed in the great concert halls along with the classics in the European canon.

What Dvořák did not point out, however, was the fact that for folk material to become a truly native fine art, it had to be extended, elaborated, and refined through the employment of devices that were also indigenous. What he either left out or failed to emphasize was the indispensable dynamics of the vernacular imperative. Those "Negro melodies" he referred to were the product not only of native folk material as such but also of a native or homegrown process, the employment of certain musical devices that were also native, if only through frontier modification of imported procedures.

Nor did Dvořák provide any example of what an original school of American composition would sound like. Certainly his *New World* Symphony was not American music. It was European music about America. It was American raw material or subject matter developed in terms of European conventions of composition. Not that any American idiom would, should, or even could be altogether different from European convention. It would be European-derived music significantly modified by conventions evolved in the Western Hemisphere.

Dvořák had heard Negro spirituals and other Negro melodies as well as the popular plantation-derived airs in the repertory of Stephen Foster to be sure, and on a visit out to Spillville, Iowa, he was impressed by various Indian melodies and chants. Moreover, between 1892 and 1894 he could also have heard ragtime tunes and cakewalk instrumentals—and perhaps also some of the new music for the fox-trot, the one-step, etc., that was beginning to replace the primacy of the waltz as the rage of popular music. Surely the composer of *Slavonic Dances* should not have missed anything so basic as that to a truly American music. Nor is it irrelevant to wonder what was or would have been his reaction to a musical element so uniquely American as syncopation.

In all events, he had returned to Europe in 1894, and he died in 1904, four years before W. C. Handy's codification of the blues put its basic structural devices in the public domain of the popular music that was to be extended, elaborated, and refined into jazz. But even so, Dvořák was prophetic enough to have declared that "in the Negro melodies of America I discover all that is needed for a great and noble school of music. They are pathetic, tender, passionate, melancholy, solemn, religious, bold, merry, gay, or what you will. It is music that suits itself to any mood or any purpose. There is nothing in the whole range of composition that cannot be supplied with themes from this source."

Among the American conservatory-oriented composers who took Dvořák's advice was William Arms Fisher, who published a book of Negro spirituals and also made an arrangement of a spiritual-derived melody from Dvořák's *New World* Symphony entitled "Going Home," which became a very popular semiclassic concert piece during the 1920s and 1930s. Another Dvořák protégé was Ruben Goldmark, who became an instructor at Mrs. Thurber's conservatory and later became the head of the Department of Composition at Julliard from 1924 until his death in 1936. One of his best-known compositions was *A Negro Rhapsody,* and among his students at one time was George Gershwin, the composer of *Rhapsody in Blue, Concerto in F, An Ameri-*

can in Paris, and *Porgy and Bess,* who also studied with a legendary Harlem stride-style piano player and composer named Luckey Roberts. Incidentally, Gershwin's pre-*Porgy and Bess* attempt to compose a Negro folk opera was called *135th Street,* a street in Harlem.

With the exception of Gershwin, such Dvořák-inspired efforts, however, did not lead to music that was significantly more peculiar to the United States than was Dvořák's own. The subject matter was indigenous, to be sure, but the process of stylization was hardly less European than his. Indeed it was as if American musical training was primarily geared to putting American subject matter into the European canon. The concert hall status of the traditional Negro spirituals and gospel and jubilee songs was obviously enhanced by Dvořák's enthusiastic admiration, but alas even they were often Europeanized by conservatory-trained musicians. After all, European conventions of stylization were precisely what American musical training was all about.

And yet within less than a generation of Dvořák's sojourn at the American conservatory there was American music that Europeans recognized as such and that had a universal appeal that was downright infectious. And it was clearly the employment of indigenous devices of stylization that led ever so sophisticated European musicians and theorists not only to admire it but also to place it in the context of avant-garde innovation rather than of the homespun or the primitive.

Obviously the keyboard skill, nay, virtuosity, required to play the ragtime piano music of Scott Joplin, for instance, was not only beyond the level of primitive and folk musicians but also beyond the precision of conservatory-trained musicians in America and Europe alike, who were very hard put indeed to reproduce the subtleties of its idiomatic nuances even after careful study and rehearsal of the scores, and the piano rolls of American musicians.

On the other hand, in the American musical context in which Duke Ellington grew up and formulated his vocational and professional objectives, the technical nuances of ragtime or Harlem stride piano were among the earliest challenges one had to learn to cope with, and as for the "Negro melodies" that so captivated Dvořák, they were as much a part of his everyday musical environment as were the idioms of everyday discourse.

Duke Ellington, né Edward Kennedy Ellington, the musician who was to become the composer who would process or stylize, which is to say extend, elaborate, and refine, more indigenous American raw material into universally appealing fine art by means of idiomatic devices than any other, was born in Washington, D.C., on April 29, 1899, six years after Dvořák's pronouncement preliminary to the premiere of the *New World* Symphony.

So in addition to the intricacies of ragtime keyboard technique as such, Ellington's musical context from the very outset of his apprenticeship (circa 1914) was one in which primary emphasis was placed on coming to terms with the vernacular music of New Orleans, the blues, vaudeville show tunes and novelties, and popular dance melodies. After all, the audiences he was hoping to please were not in the great concert, recital, and philharmonic halls. They were in the vaudeville and variety show theaters, dance halls, at parties, parlor socials, honky-tonks, after-hour joints, and dives. Moreover, Ellington always used to point out that while some of his mentors were conservatory-trained, others who were no less formidable played by ear, and that he was strongly influenced by both.

Such was the nature of the immediate context of the

beginning of the natural history of the sensibility of the musician whose idiomatic approach to composition would produce the largest body of works that amount to the musical equivalent of the representative verbal or literary anecdotes about the national character and attitudes toward life in the United States during the formative years of the twentieth century. By contrast, in most of the works of the most publicized of American concert-hall-oriented composers even such idiomatic subject matter as life in Appalachia, on the Mexican border, the world of the rodeo, or New York's Central Park, the Louisiana bayous, and the Great Plains tend to sound more like European avant-garde experimentation than the extension, elaboration, and refinement of American vernacular experience that has achieved the stylistic level of fine art. Nor does any of it amount to a significant or influential U.S. export. In any case, Ellington's music was to win a sophisticated international following even as he began to receive national recognition as a star in the area of popular entertainment in the United States.

But back to the context. As socially and politically reactionary as was the Washington of Ellington's early years of apprenticeship, it was not provincial in matters of entertainment and the arts. It was not as cosmopolitan as New York, to be sure, but even so it reflected much of the New Yorker's taste, perhaps to an extent comparable to that of a suburb of Manhattan. In fact, many Washingtonians were hardly, or only slightly, less regular patrons of New York cultural events than were residents of the five boroughs. Also, the quality of public education was such that even graduates of the outstanding segregated schools were academically qualified to satisfy the requirements of Ivy League and other elite northern colleges and universities, generally considered to be the best in the nation.

Ellington, whose academic performance in visual art qualified him for a scholarship to Pratt Institute in New York, did not graduate from high school, dropping out in his senior year to seek his fortune as a piano player in a local dance band. And yet although he never took any courses of any kind at Washington's nationally renowned Howard University, he never seemed less formally educated than those who did. Moreover, the urbane deportment of his sidemen was no less impressive than that of those in the Jimmie Lunceford Orchestra, which actually began as a student band at Fisk University, a very prestigious undergraduate liberal arts college in Nashville, Tennessee. Nor was his orientation to technical precision ever at issue. On the contrary, his band is said to have impressed other musicians as being very thoroughly rehearsed from the outset.

In all events, he never seemed to regard himself as "a young man from the provinces." And no wonder. When he and those who would become the nucleus of his great world-famous orchestra decided to go to New York and seek their fortune in the big time, they had not only heard but in a number of instances had also made personal and professional contact with such headline Manhattan-based musicians as James P. Johnson, Luckey Roberts, Eubie Blake, Fletcher Henderson, and Fats Waller, among others. After all, Washington's Howard Theater, which was more relevant to Ellington's destiny than Howard University, was not only the nearest thing in the nation to such New York T.O.B.A.-type (Theatre Owners Booking Association) circuit theaters as the Lincoln and the Lafayette, it was also the showcase for Washington's formally trained elite's cultural events.

Nor should it be forgotten that when Ellington and his musicians presented themselves to New York as the Washingtonians, they seemed to have had no fear of being mistaken for a bunch of hayseeds. Even Sonny Greer, the Manhattan-wise drummer from Long Branch, New Jersey, who had left a road show to join them several years before, seems to have had no objection to reentering the New York scene as one of the Washingtonians.

The immediate impact of Ellington on New York was not comparable to that which King Oliver, Louis Armstrong, Freddie Keppard, and other musicians from New Orleans had on the city of Chicago, but in a matter of four years he was well on his way to a prominent status in the city, the nation, and the world. Unlike the musicians from New Orleans who arrived in Chicago bringing a style of music that was not only revolutionary but immediately captivating, Ellington and his fellow musicians had come to New York to qualify as big-time professionals.

To which end, when he and his group of mostly Washingtonians that he was leading in the Hollywood Club in midtown Manhattan on Forty-ninth Street between Broadway and Seventh Avenue were booked into the plush Cotton Club nightspot uptown on Lenox Avenue at 142nd Street near the Savoy Ballroom in 1927, he had been in New York since 1923, during which time he had played in a significant variety of theaters and nightspots, including the Lafayette Theatre, Barron Wilkins' Exclusive Club, and other uptown venues, and had also made regular rounds of the legendary rent-party sessions frequented by such top-flight Harlem stride virtuoso keyboard ticklers as James P. Johnson, Luckey Roberts, Willie "the Lion" Smith, the Beetle, the Lamb, Fats Waller, and others. And there were also the tours he and his group had made in New England during which they had been enthusiastically received on the circuits played by such well-established orchestras as those of Paul Whiteman, Vincent Lopez, Coon Sanders, and Mal Hallett.

Meanwhile he had also begun to apply himself to becoming a professional writer of popular songs, and by the spring of 1925 had written the music for a revue called *Chocolate Kiddies,* the production of which featured a band led by Sam Wooding, who took it on a European tour beginning in May 1925. Also in 1924 he had begun making recordings, and by the time he began his tenure at the Cotton Club he had already recorded such enduring Ellingtonia as "East St. Louis Toodle-Oo," "Birmingham Breakdown," "Creole Love Call," and "Black and Tan Fantasy."

All of which also adds up to the definitive working context (including the competition for bookings and recording dates and sales) of the natural history of the kind of composer that Duke Ellington was to become. In New York as in the Washington of his early apprenticeship, his approach to music was not predicated on the requirements of conservatory-oriented composers of what Americans refer to as the serious music of the concert halls. It was rather the product of the immediate and daily response to and interaction with the vernacular aesthetics of the world of popular entertainment *that ranged all the way from folk-based minstrel fare through the wide variety of popular and novelty songs and the most elaborate production numbers of the more sophisticated nightclubs, hotel ballrooms, and music halls.*

Nor should it be forgotten that as a musician who was no less a performing artist than a composer, Ellington possessed a sense of context that was absolutely inseparable from his awareness of the nature of his daily and perpetual competition. Thus obviously his evolution was more directly and profoundly influenced by the approach to musical statement in the procedures involved in the output of his competition than by any established principles of formal conservatory training. In fact, in his workaday milieu many of the legitimate approaches to tone, execution, structure, and so on were often more likely to be frowned upon and derided than admired and praised.

Not that Ellington or any other major jazz musician ever hesitated to employ any conventional or so-called classical or legitimate devices that suited their needs. After all, inasmuch as the overwhelming majority of the most influential jazz musicians are musically literate, their elementary exercise books, whatever their instrument, were precisely the same as for all other formally trained musicians. The definitive idiomatic approaches and modifications of procedure were evolved and developed (extended, elaborated, and refined) as required. Such are the dynamics of the vernacular imperative to process indigenous material into aesthetic statement through the use of technical devices that are also peculiar to native procedure.

No wonder, then, that Ellington as an arranger and composer of indigenous American folk and pop music was far more directly and profoundly influenced by the output of King Oliver, Louis Armstrong, Sidney Bechet, Fletcher Henderson, and Don Redman, and by his early and indelible identification with such stride-time piano players and composers as James P. Johnson, Luckey Roberts, Willie "the Lion" Smith, and others, including such music show master craftsmen as Will Vodery, than by such highly celebrated contemporary concert hall revolutionaries as Igor Stravinsky, Béla Bartók, Claude Debussy, Erik Satie, and Maurice Ravel, or the theories of Nadia Boulanger.

Such were the background factors and workaday circumstances and incentives that actually enabled Ellington to fulfill the aspiration that led Mrs. Jeannette Thurber to bring Anton Dvořák to the United States to head an American conservatory back in 1892. Nor should the fact that Ellington's achievement was recognized by European critics before their counterparts in the United States come as any surprise either, inasmuch as it reflects the reason Mrs. Thurber sent for Dvořák in the first place.

When Ellington made his first trip abroad in 1933, such items as "East St. Louis Toodle-Oo," "Mood Indigo," "Lightnin' Louie," "Creole Love Call," and "Rockin' in Rhythm," among others, created for performance in nightclubs, dance halls, popular stage shows, popular music records, and radio broadcasts, had gained him the status of a new celebrity in the American world of popular entertainment, but he was of little or no concern to "regular" music critics and theorists in America. In Europe, however, his musicianship was regarded as a matter for serious analysis not only as quintessential American music but also as it related to contemporary European music on its own terms.

In England, for example, as Barry Ulanov reports in his biography of Ellington, Constant Lambert wrote: *"The orchestration of nearly all the numbers shows an intensely musical instinct and after hearing what Ellington can do with fourteen players in pieces like 'Jive Stomp' and 'Mood Indigo' the average modern composer who splashes about with eighty players in the Respighi manner must feel chastened. All this is clearly apparent to anyone who visits the Palladium, but what may not be so apparent is that Ellington is no mere band leader and arranger, but a composer of uncommon merit probably the first composer of real character to come out of America."*

THE EUROPEAN TRIP, during which it became quite obvious to Ellington that his approach to music was a matter of serious attention and even admiration and emulation by such highly regarded concert hall composers as Auric, Durey, Hindemith, Honegger, Poulenc, and Tailleferre, came about almost ten years before his band made its debut at Carnegie Hall in January 1943. There had been concert performances on several American college campuses during the mid 1930s, but the Carnegie Hall concert symbolized the achievement of the ultimate level of musical prestige in the United States.

Ellington, who is said to have declined an invitation to participate in the "From Spirituals to Swing" extravaganza of American folk and entertainment circuit music staged in 1938–39 by a jazz enthusiast and booster named John Hammond, certainly seems to have regarded his performance of a program of his own arrangements and compositions there as a very special historic achievement not only for his personal career but also for the idiom of American music that he represented.

So for the occasion, in addition to the premiere of *Black, Brown, and Beige,* a forty-five-minute tone parallel to the history of American Negroes, composed specifically for concert performance, the program also included such already unmistakably Ellington items as "Black and Tan Fantasy," "Rockin' in Rhythm," "Portrait of Bert Williams," "Portrait of Bojangles," "Ko-ko," "Jack the Bear," "Cotton Tail," "Boy Meets Horn," "Don't Get Around Much Anymore," and "Mood Indigo," among others.

In contrast to generally enthusiastic approval from reporters and reviewers in the realm of popular music, the so-called regular music critics, unlike a significant number of their European counterparts, tended to be condescending and dismissive, especially of *Black, Brown, and Beige.* Said one, "Such a form of composition is entirely out of Ellington's ken." As for the other selections, they were approached as if their brevity were more important than their musical content. Conspicuously absent from all the condescension, however, was any evidence of any practical understanding and appreciation of the dynamics of the evolution of national cultural identity in the arts comparable to that to be found in Constance Rourke's *American Humor: A Study of the National Character* (1931) and her posthumous *The Roots of American Culture* (1942); or in John A. Kouwenhoven's *Made in America: The Arts in Modern Civilization* (1948) and his *The Beer Can by the Highway: Essays on What's American About America* (1961).

But not only was the Carnegie Hall concert a commercial success that turned out to be the first of a series of annual "Ellington at Carnegie Hall" concerts, some previewed or repeated in comparable prestigious auditoriums in Chicago and Boston, it can also be said to have played a crucial role in making a significant number of Americans aware of the fact that a form of American music had achieved the status of fine art of universal appeal through the extension, elaboration, and refinement of folk and pop fare by means of such vernacular devices of stylization as vamps, riffs, blues choruses, pop song choruses, breaks, fills, call-and-response sequences (solo to ensemble, solo to solo, ensemble to ensemble), turnarounds, substitutions, among others, including idiomatic timbres, harmonies, elementary-level onomatopoeia (especially of the pre-diesel and electric locomotives), plus a combination of individual sensibility and skill at on-the-spot improvisation required for effective participation in a jam session.

BETWEEN THE FIRST Carnegie Hall concert in 1943 and his death in 1974 at the age of seventy-five, Ellington had gone on to compose, perform, and record such extended works, among others, as *The Deep South Suite, The Liberian Suite, A Tone Parallel to Harlem, A Tonal Group (Rhapsoditty, Fugueaditty, Jam-a-ditty), The Tattooed Bride, Night Creature, Such Sweet Thunder, Toot Suite (Red Shoes, Red Carpet, Red Garter, Ready Go), Anatomy of a Murder, The River, The Goutelas Suite, Afro-Eurasian Eclipse, New Orleans Suite,* and *The University of Wisconsin Suite.*

Shorter but no less important works such as *Main Stem, Cotton Tail, Someone, Idiom '59, Opus 69, Let the Zoomers Drool, Track 360, Satin Doll, Laying on Mellow, In a Mellotone, Sepia Panorama, C-jam Blues, B.P., Volupté, The Purple Gazelle, Afro Bossa, Black Swan,* and others not only outnumber those of any other jazz arranger/composer but also exceed them all in variety. And there are enough vocal vehicles such as "Sophisticated Lady," "Solitude," "I Let a Song Go out of My Heart," "I Got It Bad," "Rocks in My Bed," "I'm Just a Lucky So and So," "Everything but You," "Prelude to a Kiss" to qualify him as an outstanding songwriter.

WHEN LINCOLN CENTER for the Performing Arts, which includes the New York Philharmonic Orchestra, the Metropolitan Opera, the New York City Ballet, and the Julliard School, inaugurated its first year-round program of "Jazz at Lincoln Center," Duke Ellington's music was the definitive source of its approach to jazz composition, and his orchestra was the comprehensive model upon which the now internationally admired Lincoln Center Jazz Repertory Orchestra is based.

Such is the context within which "Jazz at Lincoln Center" elected to take the leading role that it played in the year-long worldwide centennial birthday celebration of Duke Ellington in 1999. During which repeated most honorable mention should also have been made of Mrs. Jeannette Thurber, who, according to an article by J. E. Vacha in the September 1992 issue of *American Heritage* entitled "Dvořák in America," "didn't merely endorse her director's theories [about the importance of "Negro melodies" in American music], she backed him up with concrete action." The same article that carried Dvořák's interview also announced her decision to open the national conservatory to black students. Tuition would be waived for the most gifted.

Two who achieved historic distinction were Harry T. Burleigh and Will Marion Cook. Burleigh, who became an outstanding singer (and who incidentally served as soloist at St. George's Episcopal Church from 1894 to 1946 and concurrently at Temple Emanu-El from 1900 to 1925), is most widely celebrated for his choral arrangements of such "classic" Negro spirituals as "Deep River," "My Lord What a Morning," "There Is a Balm in Gilead," "Were You There," "Every Time I Feel The Spirit," and "Joshua Fit the Battle of Jericho."

Will Marion Cook, who had been an outstanding young violinist at the Oberlin Conservatory and at the Berlin Hochschule, was primarily interested in composition at the National Conservatory, and he went on to collaborate with poet Paul Laurence Dunbar on *Clorindy; or, The Origin of the*

Cakewalk, a musical comedy sketch, and to write a number of other musicals on his own and with other collaborators. He also served as musical director for the legendary Williams and Walker Variety Show Company. But perhaps his most celebrated undertaking was his organization and direction of the Southern Syncopated Orchestra, which he took on a highly successful national tour in 1918 and then took to England and high acclaim in 1919.

It was Will Marion Cook (also from Washington, by the way) who was Ellington's most direct connection to Dvořák and Mrs. Jeannette Thurber. Not only did Ellington already admire him enough by 1919 to name his son Mercer Ellington after Cook's son Mercer Cook, he also sought him out in New York and began an informal mentor-and-protégé relationship that lasted until Cook's death in 1944. Incidentally, for all of his own highly impressive formal training, Cook's technical advice to Ellington was entirely consistent with the dynamics of the vernacular imperative. *Don't be restricted by the established rules. Proceed in terms of what is most natural to your own individual sensibility.* Obviously, the devices most natural to Ellington's personal *(which is to say idiomatic)* sensibility were those of ragtime, the blues, and the pop song chorus. Which suggests that as enthusiastic about American folk music as Dvořák was, he may have mistaken the vernacular devices peculiar to European musical convention for universal principles of composition. Ellington did not.

PART III | MEMOS FOR A MEMOIR

ONE | Me and Old Duke

Back in 1927, when I was eleven years old and in the fifth grade at Mobile County Training School on the outskirts of Mobile, Alabama, some twenty-plus years before Kenneth Burke's notion of art as basic equipment for living became a fundamental element in my concept of the pragmatic function of aesthetic statement, I was already trying to project myself as the storybook heroic me that I wanted to be by doing a syncopated sporty limp-walk to the patent leather avenue beat of Duke Ellington's then very current "Birmingham Breakdown."

There were also highly stylized facial expressions, gestures, postures, and other choreographic movements that went with "Mood Indigo," "Black and Tan Fantasy," and "Creole Love Call," all of which were also elements in the texture of the troposphere of that part of my preteen childhood. But "Birmingham Breakdown" (along with old Jelly Roll Morton's "Kansas City Stomp" and Fletcher Henderson's "Stampede") functioned as my personal soundtrack some years before Vitaphone movies came into being.

In junior high school there was Ellington's recording of "Diga Diga Doo," a novelty vocal that some of my classmates and I sometimes used as a cute little takeoff jive ditty on Talladega College, which, along with Morehouse College in Atlanta and Fisk University in Nashville, was a choice liberal arts college, scholarship grants to which we as honor students were already competing with each other for upon graduation. The Ellington swagger perennial from that period was "Rockin' in Rhythm."

Along with the advanced courses and grade point average competition of senior high school, plus all of the ritual challenges of full-fledged adolescence, which, by the way, included cosmopolitan standards of sartorial elegance set by the latest fashions in *Esquire,* a new men's magazine, came "It Don't Mean a Thing if It Ain't Got That Swing," "Sophisticated Lady," "Solitude," and "Delta Serenade." Although "Stormy Weather," "Cocktails for Two," and "(Everybody's) Truckin'" were not Ellington compositions, it was Ellington's arrangements and recordings that established them as radio hits and stash-swagger-fare for hip cats.

When "Caravan" came out I was in college, and that was also the year that T. E. Lawrence (of Arabia) published *Seven Pillars of Wisdom,* which eventually led me to Charles Doughty's *Travels in Arabia Deserta* and to Sir Richard Burton's *Personal Narrative of a Pilgrimage to El-Madinah & Meccah.* The dance step that used to go with "Caravan" and other ballroom exotica was the camel walk, which for a while was right out there with "Truckin'" and was no less intricate than the Suzy Q. Then came "I Let a Song Go out of My Heart" with an instrumental version that was no less popular than the lyric.

I was also in college when "Echoes of Harlem" came

out, and along with "Diminuendo and Crescendo in Blue" it as to come to represent an aesthetic statement that was more in line with my evolving sensibility and artistic aspiration than anything I had come across in *The New Negro,* Alain Locke's anthology of the so-called Harlem Renaissance.

The world I graduated into from college in 1939 was that of Count Basie's "Doggin' Around" and "Blue and Sentimental." But in 1940 came Ellington's "Cotton Tail," a musical stylization of the elegantly nimble rabbit in the briarpatch, which for me was to become the musical equivalent of a representative literary anecdote. *For example, the blues as such may be approached as the ever nimble rabbit copes with the jam-session-like challenges of the briarpatch.* Hence the name Scooter for the protagonist of *Train Whistle Guitar, The Spyglass Tree, The Seven League Boots,* and the book now in progress.

When I came to New York the first time, "Echoes of Harlem," "Uptown Downbeat," "I'm Slapping Seventh Avenue with the Sole of My Shoe," "Harlem Airshaft," and the then new "Take the A Train" had as much to do with my preconceptions and anticipations of the idiomatic texture of life in uptown Manhattan as Hollywood movies and the WPA guidebook had to do with my expectations of the great metropolis as a whole.

It was on my second visit to New York that I picked up on "Main Stem," Ellington's tone parallel to Broadway, which did for midtown Manhattan what "Harlem Airshaft" had done and still does for the special ambience of New York City above 110th Street. And as "Sepia Panorama" does for the brownskin area of every large city in the United States that I have ever visited. After all, as the old barbershop saying goes, "Nobody ever knew more about what to do with all that old chitlin circuit stuff than old Duke."

When, as a young college teacher attending graduate school at NYU, I finally met Ellington and began going to his rehearsals and recording sessions, I felt, and still feel, that what I was doing was as relevant to my career as a writer as meeting Ernest Hemingway, Thomas Mann, James Joyce, T. S. Eliot, André Malraux, William Faulkner, and W. H. Auden would have been. Incidentally, it was from Mann's application of devices of German music to prose fiction that led me to explore the existential implications of the blues and also to try to make literary applications of the devices of jazz orchestration.

In time, my personal contact with Ellington became such that he sponsored a party that his sister Ruth gave at 333 Riverside Drive at 106th Street (now renamed Duke Ellington Boulevard) when my second book, *South to a Very Old Place,* was published. And his blurb on the jacket of *Train Whistle Guitar,* my first novel, is not only the most flattering I've ever received but is also the one most often quoted in profiles and platform introductions.

But even before that, there was the fall term that I spent at Colgate University as O'Connor Professor of Literature, which was in itself an unforgettable high point in my early literary career. What made it an all but incredible time for me, however, were two other surprises. Even as I was still finding my way around the campus, *The New Yorker* magazine published a long and enthusiastic review by Robert Coles of my first book, *The Omni-Americans.* And shortly thereafter Duke Ellington himself, en route to Los Angeles where he and Ella Fitzgerald were booked into the Coconut Grove, called and said, "Hey, Albert [pronounced French style], since you have no classes between late Thursday afternoon and early next Tuesday afternoon, why not let me have our office set up a weekend round-trip flight out to L.A. I'd like to talk to you about this book that Stanley Dance and I are trying to put together."

On the flight to California, the big thrill for me was not that I was on my way to Hollywood. As an Air Force Captain assigned to duty at Long Beach Municipal Airport from 1958 to 1961, I had not only become used to driving from my residence in Compton into downtown Los Angeles and out to Hollywood to attend art exhibitions, musical entertainment and sports events as often as several times a week, I had also become a regular backstage visitor during concerts, club dates and dances every time the Ellington Band came to town. So I had also begun to go to rehearsals and recording sessions including those that produced the Ellington-Strayhorn version of *The Nutcracker Suite.*

No, the big thrill for me as I boarded the flight to Los Angeles Airport was the fact that my invitation was a follow up on a very flattering compliment that Duke had paid me two years earlier. On October 20, 1968, he had played one of his sacred concerts at Metropolitan AME church on 135th Street off Lenox Avenue, only three blocks from my apartment in Harlem. When I arrived early enough to go "backstage" to the pastor's office and study, which Duke was using as his dressing room, he introduced me to Ralph Bunche, the great United Nations diplomat. Bunche was scheduled to present Duke with a commemorative Duke Ellington postage stamp being issued by Togoland. When Duke called me over to meet Bunche, Duke told him that I was a new writer whose magazine articles were well worth checking out. "He's gone, man," he said as he turned to start dressing to go on stage, "he's already way out there."

As Bunche and I shook hands, he said "Duke's recommendation is certification enough for me." He told me about how when he, who was not a musician, was coming of age, Duke Ellington became one of his most influential role models, a development that pleased his father very much because his father thought that Ellington's cosmopolitan deportment was entirely consistent with the universality of his music.

Nor was that all. There was also the all too recent fact that when Duke's sister Ruth called from the office with specific information about transportation and lodging, she said that he had seen the very enthusiastic review of *The Omni Americans* in *Newsweek,* which also included a snapshot of me sitting beside Duke at the Newport Jazz Festival of 1961. Duke had said "It's because of cats like that I'm going to have to amount to something one of these days." I would have been just thrilled en route to meet him at a roadhouse anywhere on the chitlin' circuit.

TWO | Me and Old Uncle Billy and
the American Mythosphere

There was nothing at all avuncular about the impression he made on me when I began reading him during the first term of my freshman year at Tuskegee in the fall of 1935. At that time he, along with Ernest Hemingway, John Dos Passos, F. Scott Fitzgerald, Sherwood Anderson, Gertrude Stein, and James Joyce, and also such poets as T. S. Eliot, Ezra Pound, Archibald MacLeish, Carl Sandburg, Robert Frost, and Edwin Arlington Robinson, and such playwrights as Eugene O'Neill, Maxwell Anderson, Robert E. Sherwood, and Clifford Odets of Broadway and William Butler Yeats and John Millington Synge of the Abbey Theatre, was very much a part of what the current literary news and commentaries in newspapers and magazines in the periodicals room of the Hollis Burke Frissell Library were about.

At the time my main literary interest was drama, and

the book that led me to anthologies and surveys of world literature was *The Theatre: Three Thousand Years of Drama, Acting and Stagecraft* by Sheldon Cheney, who was also the author of *A Primer of Modern Art,* from which by that next spring I had become familiar with such aesthetic terms as Impressionism, Post-Impressionism, Cubism, Futurism, Expressionism, Dadaism, Surrealism, and so on, including Vorticism and Constructivism.

By which time, because of such weekly magazines as the *Saturday Review of Literature,* the *New York Times Book Review,* the *New York Herald Tribune Book World,* the *New Republic,* and the *Nation,* none of which had been available to me in high school, I was already spending more of my extracurricular reading time on contemporary fiction, poetry, and critical theory than on drama and stagecraft, although I was also keeping current on what was happening on the Broadway stage and on the screen and radio.

Come to think of it, although I was not really aware of it at the time, the shift of my primary reading interests from drama to prose fiction probably had already begun between mid-September and mid-November. In any case, along with Ernest Hemingway, who was writing about Florida and Cuba in sequences from *To Have and Have Not* (and also correspondence dispatch observations about the craft of fiction as such) in current issues of *Esquire* magazine, there was also one William Faulkner, whom I still remember as if it all happened yesterday. Because I will always remember the faded red print on the blue and beige binding of the Jonathan Cape–Harrison Smith edition of *These 13* that was right there on the tilted display tray at your elbow on the checkout counter in the main reading room on the second floor of the Hollis Burke Frissell Library.

So it all began with "Dry September," "Red Leaves," "That Evening Sun," "A Rose for Emily," "A Justice," and "Hair." Then came the blue-embossed sun-bleached-meadowland-beige-bound Harrison Smith–Robert Haas edition of *Light in August,* with Joe Christmas and Lena Grove and Byron Bunch and Joe Brown and Lucas Burch and Reverend Gail Hightower, Old Man McEachern, Old Doc Hines, Miss Joanna Burden, and the sheriff, plus Percy Grimm to be sure.

Then came *Absalom, Absalom!* hot off the press in 1936. *Soldiers' Pay, Mosquitoes, Sartoris, The Sound and the Fury, As I Lay Dying,* and *Sanctuary* were not available at Tuskegee at that time. John Gerald Hamilton, my favorite classmate of all times, had already read *Sanctuary* back in Detroit, his hometown, where he had also seen a movie version entitled *The Story of Temple Drake.* I don't remember him saying anything about any of the others, so I assume that he had not yet read any of them either, because I can't imagine him not saying anything about the stylistic innovations that Faulkner employed in the Benjy and Quentin sections of *The Sound and the Fury,* and I still think about how much fun it would have been to have him there with his input on the decoding of those first 222 pages. What with him already checked out as he alone among the undergraduates I knew was on such contemporary writers as James Joyce and Marcel Proust and such stylistic innovations in narration as the stream of consciousness, the fourth dimension, free association, imagism, symbolism, and so on.

Which, of course, is why both *Light in August* and *Absalom, Absalom!* were so much easier going for him than for me. But I was no less captivated even so. And I still think of both (which I reread immediately) as belonging as much to me as to anybody. Incidentally, the fact that the current reviews of *Absalom, Absalom!* were hardly laudatory had no negative affect on our enthusiasm whatsoever. Both novels were like tunes you keep humming to yourself because you like them for yourself regardless of what anybody else thinks.

Hamilton was back up north when *The Unvanquished* arrived in 1938. So I made what I made of the Civil War and Reconstruction escapades of Bayard Sartoris and Ringo on my own. But there was something about the curiosity that the two of them shared and the running-mate games they played that reminded me time and again of how things were when he was there. Young Bayard Sartoris was no Huck Finn to be sure. Although in some ways he and Ringo were personally closer than Huck and Jim (who, after all, was an adult, not Huck's age peer). And I had serious doubts about the naïveté of Ringo's devotion to the Confederacy. But Faulkner's rendering of Ringo's competitive curiosity and self-confident ingenuity are not condescending, and his account of Ringo's efforts to conceive the concrete image of a functioning railroad train, something he not only has never heard of before Bayard comes back from a trip and tells him about one but has nothing to compare it with, is as profoundly insightful as it is hilarious.

And yet, as far as I know, Faulkner never got around to coming to terms with an emancipated and reconstructed Ringo. There was the formidable Lucas Beauchamp of *Go Down, Moses* and *Intruder in the Dust* to be sure, and several others not unlike him who exemplify the traditional orientation to the dignified bearing and noble aspirations of their "high-class" white relatives in the Edmonds, McCaslin, and Sartoris families. But what about the ex-slaves, mulatto or not, who became leaders, teachers, professionals, and businessmen? The Reconstruction was not a farce, nor was it mostly a disaster perpetrated by corrupt carpetbaggers. In spite of the widespread hostility and all of the horrendous acts of terrorism by the likes of Nathan Bedford Forrest and others, the transition from freedom from slavery to responsible U.S. citizenship and unimpeachable patriotism is unexcelled by any other stories of the making of any other Americans.

THE LAST FAULKNER NOVEL I read before graduating from Tuskegee in 1939 was *The Wild Palms,* in which the nightmarish Old Man River flood story came across very effectively in spite of the way it was seemingly arbitrarily interwoven with the totally different narrative sequences of the Harry Wilbourne–Charlotte Rittenmeyer fiasco, the implications of which became richer later on when I eventually got around to reading Faulkner's New Orleans-based equivalent to the influential 1920s *Wasteland*-oriented efforts of the poet T. S. Eliot, the novelist F. Scott Fitzgerald, and others in such books as *Soldiers' Pay, Mosquitoes, Pylon,* and *New Orleans Sketches.* Then very belatedly there was also *Sartoris (Flags in the Dust)* for all its benchmark status in the Yoknapatawpha chronicles.

William Faulkner's stylization of the idiomatic particulars of the Deep South is very much a part of what impressed me about his fiction from the very outset. Moreover, even then it was not simply a matter of regional or provincial atmosphere or local color, not as such. Even then there was something about it that had the effect of transforming all too familiar everyday down-home environmental and demographic details into the stuff of poetry, the stuff that the so-called avant-garde poetry of T. S. Eliot, Ezra Pound, e. e. cummings, Marianne Moore, and Robinson Jeffers, among others, was made of.

For me, the "mot juste" prose of Ernest Hemingway's *In Our Time* and *The Sun Also Rises* was also the stuff of such poetic endeavor. But whereas the poetry of Hemingway's prose struck me as being all-American in a Walt Whitmanesque sense (also with overtones of syndicated wire service vernacular to be sure), Faulkner's Southerners' linguistic southernness, not unlike the unmistakably Irish idiom of James Joyce's Dubliners, was no less potentially international in its avant-garde chicness and already no less immediate in the universality of its implications. *(For me, at any rate, what André Malraux made of* Sanctuary *recalls what Baudelaire and the French made of Poe!)* Stylization could make small-town down-home stuff, even Mississippi small-town down-home stuff, as universal as anything from anywhere else.

Also, when I think of the near-symphonic orchestral convolution of some of Faulkner's prose as compared with the streamlined precision of Ernest Hemingway's Kansas City Star-*disciplined 4/4-like incantation, it is as if Faulkner were a not-quite-not-Thomas-Sutpen Mississippi planter and occasional-riverboat-to-New-Orleans dandy and sometime gentleman rider-huntsman who inhabits a haunted antebellum mansion on what is left of a vast plantation inherited from ancestors whose accruals were derived directly from owning and exploiting human slaves. Some of them very close relatives indeed. A prop-laden stage set for costume drama with ever so historical resonances.*

Whereas for me, it was as if Hemingway's style was that of some species of an all-American sportsman in leotards on a clean, well-lighted, starkly symbolic, multilevel stage set for ritual sketches. And of course much goes to show that it is the ritual sketch that the costume drama, however elaborate, must add up to. Which well may be as good a reason as any why "The Bear" in Go Down, Moses may be regarded as a crucial if not definitive Faulkner achievement.

No, there was nothing about the impression that William Faulkner made on me during those early years that was as yet avuncular. But even so, he had become Old Faulkner almost as fast as Little Louis Armstrong had become Old Louis and the handsome young Duke Ellington had become Old Duke. That was because at a very early age he had his own way of doing what he did that commanded the serious attention and respect not only of his peers but also of his elders as well. Indeed what it meant was that he was already on his way to becoming an elder himself. Because there was something about the way that he did what he did that left you more bemused and/or astonished and impressed than aghast and outraged. In any case, I submit that he had already become Old Faulkner early on because it was already so obvious that he was headed for the status of the legendary and, who knows, perhaps eventually the status of a classic.

As an undergraduate I associated the idiomatic particulars of Faulkner's role as a regional elder in the arts with what I regarded as a post-Confederate southern small-town seed store, feed store, courthouse square sensibility. Not that I had any firsthand experience of such places. I had grown up hearing fireside tales, tall and otherwise, about such potentially explosive southern small towns as Atmore, Bay Minette, Flomaton, and so on in Alabama. But Magazine Point, where I spent the first nineteen years of my life, was a small suburb of the international seaport city of Mobile, whose downtown municipal and business center we were directly connected to by a trolley car ride of only a matter of perhaps thirty minutes or less and a shortcut walk of less than an hour. So the small courthouse square Macon County seat of Tuskegee was actually my very first ongoing contact with a small courthouse square town with a Confederate statue like Faulkner's town of Jefferson. So Jefferson was just as real as Tuskegee town, and the town of Tuskegee was just as much a part of a storybook world as Faulkner's Jefferson.

In all events, when as a graduate whose literary context by that time included Thomas Mann, André Malraux, James Joyce, Marcel Proust, Arthur Koestler, Ignazio Silone, and Franz Kafka, among others, and such poets as Auden, Spender, and C. Day-Lewis, I came back around to reading Faulkner when *The Hamlet* and then *Go Down, Moses* were published, my image of the idiomatic dimension of him as a Deep South elder became that of a book-oriented corn-whiskey-drinking cracker-barrel lie swapper and hot-stove yarn spinner, whose cosmopolitan literary awareness was as natural to him as was his comprehensive courthouse square awareness of local, regional, national, and global affairs. None of which seemed to have very much if anything to do with drawing room chic but was clearly of a piece with the nuts-and-bolts stuff of local politics and ever so confidential inside gossip. And thus perhaps not a little to do with the motives underlying narrative action.

It was when he became more and more involved with the Snopes people and the Varners that I realized that, along with everything else that had made him Old Faulkner, there was also something that made him Old Uncle Billy as far as I was personally concerned. My having grown up in the Deep South as I had, he was my own personal very special big-house equivalent to and literary extension of my traditional brownskin fireside, barbershop, and storefront loafers rest-bench Uncles Bud, Doc, Ned, Pete, and Remus (with pipe sometimes alternating with cigar).

Because just as it was as if old Uncles Bud, Doc, Ned, Pete, and Remus existed to make you aware of attitudes, acts, and implications that you were not yet old enough to come by on your own for all your ever alert and even ingenious curiosity, so were old Uncle Billy's books there to pull you aside and provide you with inside insights not readily available to you as an everyday matter of course, because you were neither white nor a personal servant.

So the quest for universality in aesthetic statement being what it is, and despite his avowed but ambivalent desire for anonymity, Old Faulkner became and still is my very own idiomatic old Uncle Billy. Not for all intents and purposes to be sure, but for quite a few even so. In all events, anywhere his concerns and curiosity took him I could go also, and so can you. For such is indeed the nature and function of literary artistic endeavor in the human scheme of things.

Thus what William Faulkner's avuncular status with me comes down to is precisely the role of the literary artist in the contemporary American mythosphere, a term I am appropriating from my friend Alexander Eliot. In other words, there is the physical atmosphere of planet Earth which is said to extend some six hundred miles out into space in all directions and consists of the troposphere in which we live, and beyond which is the stratosphere, beyond which are the mesosphere, the ionosphere, and exosphere.

The mythosphere is that nonphysical but no less actual

and indispensable dimension of the troposphere in which and in terms of which human consciousness exists, and as we all know, the primary concern of all artistic endeavor is the quality of human consciousness, whether our conception of things is truly functional, as functional as a *point or moral* of the classic fables and fairy tales. But that is quite a story in itself. Let me just say that I assume that the role of the serious literary artist is to provide mythic prefigurations that are adequate to the complexities and possibilities of the circumstances in which we live. In other words, to the storyteller actuality is a combination of facts, figures, and legend. The goal of the serious storyteller is to fabricate a truly fictional legend, one that meets the so-called scientific tests of validity, reliability, and comprehensiveness. Is its applicability predictable? Are the storyteller's anecdotes truly representative? Does his "once upon a time" instances and episodes imply time and again? I have found that in old Uncle Billy's case they mostly do.

PART IV | BOOK REVIEWS

ONE | The HNIC Who He

Many white people may always seem only too eager to seize upon any explanation that traces the Negro Revolution to some single source of motivation. But when you come right down to it nobody in the United States is actually convinced that when you have heard one Negro you have heard them all—any more than anybody has ever really believed that once you have seen one you have seen them all. Nevertheless, somebody who knows very well that there is no single spokesman for anybody else is forever asking somebody to tell him who speaks for the Negro!

When somebody approaches and says, "Take me to your leader," a Negro is faced with the same problem as other Americans. All anybody has to do is glance at the headlines or switch on the television to find out that there are not only a lot of different Negroes to be spoken for but also a lot of different ones who are not about to let anybody else speak for them.

No one can deny that the resulting confusion is often exasperating. But neither can any responsible American dispute the fact that such diversity, *although it sometimes becomes downright chaotic,* is a normal and inevitable outcome of the freedom of speech. Hence, not only do Negroes have as much right to dissent from each other as from Whitey, they are as likely to do so in any case. Moreover, as Harold Cruse obviously assumed when he undertook *The Crisis of the Negro Intellectual,* the only realistic thing to do is come to practical terms with it.

Such, at any rate, is the indispensable requirement that this book fulfills. Indeed, in the process of establishing what is by all odds the most imaginatively documented and politically sophisticated working prospective on the built-in contradictions and disjunctions of the Negro Revolution up to now, he has written the most urgently needed if not the most important book of the year.

There will be some quibbling over details, to be sure, and certainly there are going to be a number of furious people with exposed and tingling backsides. But they had better get it all together before they lash back at Harold Cruse. Many Negro writers either shirk or shuck on intellectual matters. Not him. He takes care of business. But let us hope that a great number of general readers and intellectuals as well will be quick to realize that *The Crisis of the Negro Intellectual* adds a long-overdue dimension to the national dialogue on the nature and implications of racial and cultural pluralism.

Most other Negro writers still rely on the same old easy devices that make white people feel so deliciously defensive and guilty—only because they also make them feel so powerful. Cruse, who is as thoroughly checked out on militant protest as the next black brother, expresses his often brilliant insights into the political and cultural implications of Negro experience on the highest level of intellectual abstraction, against the broadest and richest historical background, and always with a practical eye on the possibilities of implementation.

Also unlike most other Negro writers, who almost always allow fatherly white spokesmen to set up the same old context within which Negro aspirations will be interpreted and considered, Cruse establishes his own frame of reference. He makes his own historical and ideological assessments and reevaluations and derives his own point of view. Thus his working conception of cultural black nationalism does not fit into any of the oversimplified categories now being popularized by mass media.

In consequence, his carefully documented observations on the development of Harlem as culture capital, on the differences between U.S. Negroes and West Indian Negroes, on Negroes and Jews, Negroes and left-wingers, and so on, should make truly concerned Americans realize just how little useful information most of the reporters and social science experts have been able to give them about the so-called Negro community.

The Burden of Race, edited by Gilbert Osofsky, the author of *Harlem: The Making of a Ghetto,* is a compilation of documents and short articles that expose once more the horrors of white racism and black victimization. Given a publisher's contract, any fairly competent Negro college librarian could get one up in a couple of weeks. The minute someone other than a Negro has the same batch of clippings done up as a book, however, he is immediately accepted by the Do-good Foundations as having qualified as a scholarly authority, panelist, and consultant on black miseries.

The titles and commentaries of *The Burden of Race* only

reiterate what Osofsky's first book had made clear enough: he has no business being promoted into black experthood for the simple reason that he has nothing significant to say about Negro experience. Negroes already have enough burdens without being saddled with any more cliché-nourished, Stanley M. Elkins-oriented theorists who insist on confusing them with Jews.

No one is likely to accuse Budd Schulberg of trying to become the Great White Jewish Father and Spokesman for Watts. But the voices he has chosen for audition in *From the Ashes* make it only too clear that the writers' workshop he set up there after the riot of 1965 is based on the same old sentimental liberal conception of the making of the wailing-wall spokesman. The establishment of Douglass House as an experiment in vocational education proves that Schulberg cares about giving the downtrodden a break. But the quality of the writing in *From the Ashes* does not indicate that he either cares or even knows as much about developing first-rate writers. No white coach bent on finding first-rate Negro athletes would ever allow himself to be faked so far out of position.

Most of the sketches, stories, verses, and various works in progress that Schulberg has so generously included in this anthology are not only pretty dull but also embarrassingly square. Not because any of the writers lack the necessary intelligence or potential but because they are so woefully "not yet with" what big-league literature is really all about. Evidently Schulberg has failed to tell them that they're writing not like John Coltrane and after, but like way before Dixieland. Schulberg became so turned-on caring about people and encouraging them to tell it like it nitty-gritty is that he forgot that writing is an artistic process. It involves the creation of significant form, which is always derived from some other form. Thus, no matter how much suffering, injustice, or anything else young writers have personally undergone, what their writing is likely to begin reflecting is not the pulsating actuality of raw experience but rather what they have been able to make of their *reading* experience.

Had Schulberg not forgotten about the writers he had worshiped and imitated in the process of finding himself as a writer, he might have noticed that Watts musicians, who are not any better off economically or socially, are infinitely more sophisticated about great musicians and the world of music at large than his writers seem to be about literature.

This acknowledged, Schulberg may also have realized something else: young people who really and truly aspire to be serious writers are hooked on books as musicians are hooked on records and painters are hooked on museums. They just simply do not stuff around waiting for some best-selling novelist to suffer an attack of brotherhood fever and come out and start corralling them in from the sidewalks. Poverty does not kill young writers any faster in Watts than in Paris or in Greenwich Village—and it doesn't force them to be any farther out of things than it forces musicians to be. Item: No other young musicians anywhere in the world were up any tighter with what was happening in their chosen profession than were Charlie Mingus, Buddy Collette, and Chico Hamilton when they came out of Watts.

Perhaps it is through just such a realization that Schulberg may still find the clue to a more effective workshop. He might do well to begin with another conception of poetic license. Freedom of expression does not come from ignoring great books but from reading as many as possible and thus increasing one's range of awareness. Writers do not discover themselves by studying their own belly buttons but by realizing what they like and dislike about other writers. Aspiring Negro writers must be made aware of the mainstream of contemporary expression if only to reject it.

But the chances are that once they really dig the literary scene, black writers will begin playing the same highly imaginative improvisations on the works of James Joyce, Thomas Mann, Proust, Malraux, Hemingway, Faulkner, T. S. Eliot, Auden, Dylan Thomas, and Robert Lowell that the Harlem Globetrotters play with "the white man's" basketball, and Willie Mays plays with "the white man's" baseball, and Sugar Ray used to play with "the white man's" boxing gloves and Jim Brown with "the white man's" pigskin. Nor should the current emphasis on "black consciousness" be allowed to obscure the fact that neither Lester Young nor Charlie Parker compromised his blackness because he played "the white man's" saxophone. As for the integrity and the potential of Negro writers, anybody who begins by assuming that they won't learn to play their own riffs of *Finnegans Wake* just simply has never really listened to them talk.

Stokely Carmichael often sounds much more like a black prince making decrees for a nation of gullible black subjects than like one black spokesman among many others. Perhaps that's why white image-makers have always confused his rise with the Return of Emperor Jones. In any case, when he appears on television (sometimes in costume) chanting rhymes and slogans, white people have been only too quick to regard him as a part of show biz. Not many will mistake *Black Power* for entertainment.

The polemic which he has written with Charles V.

Hamilton of Roosevelt University is not only serious, it is furious. It states his case for black radical political action; and it is a stimulating and useful political manifesto in spite of his same old bewildering reliance on undigested theories and superficial oversimplification. If only black activists would get off that Instant Mass Psychiatry kick! If only they would do more homework in general culture and remember the richness of their actual experience with black complexity and become less glib with fancy jargon. If activists really concur with the current social science conjectures about black emasculation and self-hatred, they cannot possibly believe that Negroes are now ready for revolt. But Negroes are ready. And they didn't get that way overnight.

There are any number of techniques that black revolutionaries can use to undermine the symbols of white authority. But instead of exposing and ridiculing the personal weaknesses and insecurities of white individuals and the hysteria of white masses, most Negro spokesmen almost always spend most of their time inflating the efficiency of the White Power Structure while reinforcing all of the clichés of black wretchedness. A short seminar on white pathology with a few old insightful black headwaiters, bell-boys, maids, and Pullman porters might be as useful to black insurgence as the hypotheses of Marx, Freud, and Frantz Fanon.

But then the fact that Carmichael literally cringes when white people describe Negroes as lazy, shiftless, apathetic good-timers shows how taken in by "white middle-class values" he still is. If not, why not insist that black laziness and shiftlessness have been forms of subversive resistance since slavery; that black apathy really represents a profound rejection of the white "rat race," and that black good times only go to show what wonderful human beings U.S. Negroes are in spite of white brutality.

Black Power zings with urgent black concern about black welfare. But for all their repeated references to black consciousness, Carmichael and Hamilton, unlike the author of *The Crisis of the Negro Intellectual,* often sound like white do-gooders speaking through black masks. So much so that you get the uneasy feeling that in spite of themselves they might be confusing human dignity with white middle-class norms and suburban respectability. But their observations on white political double-dealings and black social imperatives may just prove to be enough to take care of the business they really have in mind. After all, U.S. Negroes often turn the flimsiest pop tunes into some of the richest music in the world.

TWO | Soul Brothers Abroad

The typical immigrant arriving in New York can hardly wait to be naturalized. His fantasies about being in the United States almost always include playing an active role as a full-fledged citizen. Seldom is there a comparable eagerness for such commitment to an alien land on the part of Americans who settle elsewhere. The vast majority never give up their American citizenship; and among those who do, only a few ever become as integrated into civic activities as they were in the United States. In truth, the stateside internationalist often seems more involved with the fortunes of France and Italy than most Americans who have lived in Paris and Rome for decades.

Most of those whose observations Ernest Dunbar records in *The Black Expatriates*, a book of interviews with U.S. Negroes living in Europe and Africa, conform to the pattern of their fellow countrymen abroad. But as anyone could guess, there are also some significant differences. One is the ostensible reason for living abroad. All of the Negroes interviewed cite racism in America. White expatriates, of course, rarely give racism as a reason for exile—although the psyches of most whites are terribly scarred by the role, active or passive, they play in the exploitation of black Americans.

On the other hand, hardly any Negroes have departed in disgust at the emptiness of American materialism. Unlike the white expatriate, who is forever reiterating his renunciation of a system which was trying to shrink him to a meaningless cipher, the Negro émigré—even the artist—always seems resentful precisely because he was spurned by the selfsame system. What everybody in *The Black Expatriates* seems most concerned about is not the furious banality of the rat race back home, but how to become an acknowledged part of it.

In his introduction, Dunbar claims that for many Negroes the resolution of "problems of identity" and the "battle for integration" are complicated by black "rejection of some of the dominant values of white America." Granted. But the only "white" value his interviewees complain about is preferential treatment. Otherwise, time and again they carry on as if there would be no problem of identity or anything else if Negroes were accepted by white Americans.

In spite of all the unmistakable evidence in the arts (not to mention psychiatric case histories) and all the social chaos and political bankruptcy, most of Dunbar's black expatriates seem downright oblivious to the fact that white Americans are having infinitely more trouble identifying themselves than Negroes have ever had. The widely admired and imitated U.S. Negro idiom in music, dance, social deportment, and even food either means that there is a U.S.

Negro cultural tradition—and hence context for identity—or it means nothing! Significantly, the black exiles' nostalgia for down-home cooking (not hot dogs and hamburgers) remains strong.

The people in *The Black Expatriates* know very well who they are and what they want, but they confuse self-realization with mass-media publicity. (A rich and famous white musician, for example, does not automatically have more *identity* than an obscure Negro whose material he has appropriated.) Nevertheless, as a book about how to become more American by going overseas, *The Black Expatriates* makes interesting reading.

And so does *Where To, Black Man?*, which has drawn from a diary Ed Smith kept during his two years in Ghana with the Peace Corps. A Negro from Alabama by way of Chicago and elsewhere, Smith is not an expatriate. He is an active idealist with keen literary as well as journalistic insight. Thus his book is, among other things, a much needed antidote for some of the racist nonsense currently fashionable among "African bag" hipsters. "No," he writes of Ghana, "I shouldn't think that the Afro-American has much call to feel secure here: I'll bet when the axe of Africanization falls, white *and* black outsiders will find their wings clipped."

THREE | Freedom Bound U.S.A.

Those Negroes and those ever so liberal, completely compassionate, but very white friends of the Negro who are so readily convinced that they must look beyond the shores of the United States to find a great and honorable tradition of Negro heroism are obviously unacquainted with the extraordinary studies in Americana which have been made by Henrietta Buckmaster, the author of *Freedom Bound*. This is unfortunate, for Miss Buckmaster's work contains indispensable information about the *actual* history of Negroes in this nation, a subject about which most present-day liberals and those very special Negroes they befriend seem to know so little that one can only wonder what they really know and truly *understand* about the nation itself. It is extremely difficult to believe that they could possibly understand very much that is of fundamental significance. For since there never was a time when *freedom* was not a basic issue in the United States, there never was a time since 1619 when Negroes were not a basic issue.

One also wonders where their conception of heroism comes from in the first place. They insist that they are searching for a heritage of honor and pride and courage and devotion to human dignity and freedom. But when they also persist in ignoring so much of the flesh-and-blood history all around them at home and go chasing off to beat the Herskovitsian underbrush along some African riverbank, their very procedure destroys that which they claim they are seeking, and besides, nothing that they might find in Africa could possibly be as significant as what they have overlooked in Dismal Swamp, Virginia.

There are homegrown Negroes who are the very embodiment of all that has ever qualified anybody for heroism. They are in fact beyond number. They are found in every section of the country. And they always have been there.

The very first American to shed his blood in defense of liberty at the battle of Bunker Hill was Crispus Attucks, a Negro, who fell before the British foe on the first assault. Most very white patriots seem never to have heard of him. On the other hand, every U.S. schoolchild, very white, very black, brown, and beige, not only remembers but reveres Patrick Henry for merely *saying,* "Give me liberty or give me death!" It is enough to make one wonder just how much of this national hero business is really kid stuff after all.

Crispus Attucks was only one of scores of Negroes, freedmen and slaves alike, known to have served with great distinction during the Revolution even while the "problem" of their enlistment was still being debated in the Continental Congress. (It is also forgotten that white men could substitute Negroes to do their military service, and did. But that is a whole story in itself, and there is still another story in the scores of slaves who deserted to the British, who promised them freedom.) During the war of 1812 thousands fought again after having been promised emancipation for doing so. This promise, by the way, which had also been made during the Revolutionary War, was generally forgotten as soon as the war was over. Forgotten? The legal protection of slavery was made tighter! And after each war many Negroes who had been granted freedom for military service were pressed back into bondage.

But even during the days of the middle passage there were *Amistads* and Cinqués; and during the two hundred years of slavery there were more than three hundred known slave uprisings large and small. There just simply never was a time when U.S. Negroes were not performing daring feats in quest of freedom.

And as for the fugitive slave—and there were thousands upon thousands of him—what other national figures does one place above him man for man? Who at Jamestown? Who on the Mayflower? Who at Valley Forge? Who at Vicksburg or Gettysburg? What mythological heroes? What fairy tale heroes, even?

There is no need to minimize the justly celebrated exploits of the backwoodsman, the keel boatman, and the prairie schoonermen (among whom, incidentally, there were also Negroes, and not unusually), but given the difference in circumstances, equipment, and, above all, *motives,* these exploits become relatively *safe.* When one sets them beside the breathtaking adventures of the runaway slave beating his way south to Florida, to the West and the Indians, to faraway Canada, God knows how, through swamp and town alike, to freedom. Daniel Boone has been immortalized for finding his way through the wilderness to Tennessee, but remember *nobody* was chasing him. The fugitive slave not only qualifies as a national hero, he was an epic hero if ever there was one, and he came a dime a dozen. But so far the very laws which were enacted against him have been his only official tribute.

And yet all of this will come as incredible news to most very patriotic Americans. And among them will be found a staggering number of "good" teachers from the very best white schools. That every stripe of bigot will manifest this exasperating ignorance is to be expected, but so will an astonishing number of people of demonstrated goodwill. One had not thought segregation had undone so much in so many ways.

None of this (information), however, and none of its implications will come as a surprise to Henrietta Buckmaster, who is not one of those overtime friends of the Negro and the ghetto Indian, thank goodness. She is, more fundamentally, a friend of freedom, a friend of the rights of man, and therefore not only a friend but also a champion of the American Republic as the last best hope on earth. She is also a friend of journalistic accuracy and academic responsibility.

A number of years ago she made the shocking discovery that "nine out of ten" U.S. historians were guilty of ignoring, omitting, distorting, and even suppressing information about the Negro, and set about putting the record straight. The research involved was exciting enough in itself. The world she discovered *was the very essence of adventure and romance.*

The first result of her findings was a superbly rendered popular account of the Underground Railroad and the growth of the abolition movement which was published in 1941. It was called *Let My People Go* and has already become something of a classic on that subject. This book alone resurrected enough heroes Negro and white to fill a special national pantheon.

And speaking of representative men, it is Frederick Douglass, an ex-slave, who by any and all standards of essential worth to the nation deserves a place near Lincoln as the finest example of a nineteenth-century American, not Robert E. Lee. Schoolchildren should be told the truth. Robert E. Lee was a *Confederate* general. He fought *against* the Union. He was a *traitor.* His armies did their very best to *defend human slavery.* This was *bad.* He was *very* bad. He was *un-American.* Frederick Douglass was all-American. He championed the rights of all men. This is what the United States stands for, not the lost cause of special privilege. How utterly confusing all the hypocrisy and subversive sentimentality about Robert E. Lee must be to newly arrived immigrants and *their* children! Or is this just the sort of thing which makes European refugees realize that the simple oath of allegiance puts them one up on all native-born U.S. Negroes in so many ways?

Freedom Bound is Henrietta Buckmaster's current book. It is a relatively brief but fairly comprehensive and vividly documented summary of events immediately following the Civil War, and again she has had to set the record straight. For the image of U.S. Negroes during this critical era has not only been misrepresented, it has been defiled. In fact, no other period in U.S. history has been more systematically falsified to justify racism, segregation, and the political doctrine of white supremacy.

Consequently the average American, even today, still thinks of the Reconstruction as having been ill advised if not downright sinister and even degenerate at its very inception. This same sometimes well-meaning American is also likely to *concede* that the Reconstruction program was at any rate foredoomed by completely unscrupulous Yankee carpetbaggers and thoroughly corrupt local scalawags who used totally and inherently unfit Negroes to add insult to injury as they plundered the prostate but gallant South.

The facts are otherwise. Never in history has a defeated enemy received such *generosity* from the victors. Those who had tried to destroy the Union were back in the Union with an incredible amount of power and privilege in six weeks' time and were allowed to continue the old fight by all means short of formal declaration of war! As for the Reconstruction program itself, it was designed to convert the freedman *and the poor white* into productive citizens. Property confiscated toward this end, it should be remembered, had already been *won* in the battle. *After all, the owners could have been shot as traitors.*

As for the Negro politician of that day, *Freedom Bound* cites instance after instance to show that not only was he as well qualified as the general run of his white colleagues in many ways, his credentials were outstanding. And at any rate, the measures which he supported were not only worthwhile but also in the best interests of the nation at large. Ironically enough, one has only to indicate the key role the Negro politician (and voter) played in bringing *universal suffrage, public education,* and *public health services* to the South, an indispensable role which he played consciously.

But then heroism, when it is tragic heroism—which is certainly what this was—always involves irony. On the other hand, it is not only ironic but downright ludicrous when present-day white northern liberals who never heard of the nearly two hundred thousand Negroes who fought in the Union army, to say nothing of the work many of the veterans did with the Freedman's Bureaus, presume to teach U.S. Negroes self-respect. In thick accents yet, *mamma mia, nein,* comrade! How many white American voters have ever faced the threats of overwhelming terror the Negro voters braved during the Reconstruction? Thousands of unintimidated Negroes were murdered, ambushed, massacred on their way to and from polling places during one seven-year period.

The Reconstruction was not a golden age. Not by any means. It failed. But not only can current civil rights leaders look with frank pride at the statute of the remarkable predecessors in whose great footsteps they follow, they should aspire to be as bold. They should hope to have visions as broad. They should seek to maintain as much integrity under fire.

The nineteenth-century U.S. Negro leader did not take his cues from tax-exempt charitable organizations. He welcomed assistance of course. But he also insisted on his own definitions and he never ceased to *demand* his rights. He had traveled the Underground Railroad, had been through the Civil War; he knew very well what all of the shooting was about, and he had never really regarded the United States as being the white world, even during slavery. He thought of it as a land of incomparable opportunity for *free* men, and he was right.

Neither did he waste very much of his time on any nonsense about Negritude and the whole complex continent of Africa. He was much too busy with such immediate things as the everyday bread-and-butter matters of U.S. citizenship for that. Few freedmen went back to Africa after emancipation. Far more came back "home" from Canada. Most were here to stay and had always known it, and many among them were actively engaged to run things. Hiram Revels, for instance, became U.S. senator from Mississippi, filling the seat vacated by Jefferson Davis. James Rapier and Jerimiah Haralson went to Congress from Alabama, and in Washington they met many Negro politicians from other states. There were Negroes elected to the legislatures in most southern states, and in South Carolina, Mississippi, and Louisiana they became lieutenant governors. P. B. S. Pinchback became governor of Louisiana for a short time. And so on and on it went.

These men were seldom faked off-balance by disguised theories of race or ideology. It took betrayal on a national scale and wholesale terrorism and outright murder unparalleled in U.S. history to reduce them to second-class citizenship. They were never reduced to second-class men. In a very special sense the last of these men were still around until Jack Johnson died in an automobile accident in 1946.

Somebody is forever and ever reminding U.S. Negroes that they need allies. Perhaps they do, although the reminder is itself obscenely racist in its implications. All causes need allies. Genuine allies. But U.S. Negroes most emphatically do not need a bunch of misinformed, misdirected, self-indulgent white creeps and silly billies fouling up the atmosphere with a lot of nitwit definitions and generalizations from Marx and Freud without the slightest awareness of the basic issues, the political realities, or the actual historical context of the struggle itself.

U.S. Negroes certainly do need more white "allies" who will take the time to study and try to understand what *American Negroes* are all about, who can identify with their glories and therefore truly empathize with their defeats.

They can use many more people like Henrietta Buckmaster. But then she is not really so very white as she is a responsible and very much engaged fellow citizen, and after all, the nation needs her freedom-based heroes as much as Negroes do.

FOUR | The Good Old Boys
Down Yonder

To some people the special breed of ever so colorful white Southerners that Paul Hemphill recom-
mends as the good old boys are likely to be nobody
but the same old too-familiar hateful-eyed, razor-backed,
lynch-mob-prone, willfully backward, hysterically insecure,
but undeniably gritty peckerwoods, hillbillies, crackers, red-
necks, Hoosiers, and swamp crawlers once thought to be
the primary antagonists of civil rights. To others they will
no doubt suggest nothing so much as William Faulkner's
brass-stealing, barn-burning, horse-trading, manure-tracking,
but no less shrewd than persistent Snopeses of *The Hamlet,
The Town,* and *The Mansion.* Indeed, in Hemphill's own
words, they represent a "mean, half-educated, vengeful,
regressive" side of the South, and the world could very well
do without it.

But for Hemphill, who grew up as one of them (or, perhaps more precisely, as the son of one of them), they also represent something "distinctive and good," a spirit and a style that gives him a "sense of place" that eludes him in such unsavory whereabouts as New York and the Philadelphia of Grace Kelly (of Monaco?). As good old Louis Armstrong once did about the blues, he allows as how if you don't already know what a good old boy is, you never will. But it is easy enough to see that he is talking about a special kind of self-styled and even wrongheaded personal integrity that he for one associates with hard-drinking, hell-raising, chance-taking truck drivers, good old sheriffs (!), baseball bums, country singers, and stock car racers, among others, whose motto is probably: "Hang in there, old buddy."

Paul Hemphill himself is a journalist from Alabama by way of Georgia, the *Atlanta Journal,* and the Harvard of Neiman Fellows. He is also the author of *The Nashville Sound,* a book about country music. *The Good Old Boys* is a collection of newspaper and magazine articles about the South in the late 1950s and early 1970s, and he says it is intended more or less as an epitaph.

To be sure. Even as he reconciles himself to the inevitability of the extensive changes that have brought better housing, food, education, and race relations to the South, his mood becomes elegiac: "The Good Old Boys are out in the suburbs now, living in identical houses and shopping at the Kmart and listening to Glenn Campbell (Roy Acuff and Ernest Tubb are too tacky now) and hiding their racism behind code words. They have forfeited their style and their spirit, traded it all in on a color TV and Styrofoam beams for the den, and I find them about as exciting as reformed alcoholics."

In other words, as full of a "sense of place" as he becomes when he remembers the South from elsewhere, and for all his folk-hero-worshipful protestations, when Hemphill actually gets down to cases he finds very little left to celebrate. The good old boys, like the good old days during which they came into being, are something else southern that is mostly gone with the wind: "No more tent revivalists blowing through town like rainmakers," he laments at another point. "No more fat-bellied sheriffs fleecing the Yankees out on U.S. 1. No more Crackers double-parking in front of the Grand Old Opry House and coming out later with a contract. No more Governors with the audacity to tell the multitude that they have three friends: 'God, Sears & Roebuck and Eugene Talmadge.'" And so on. No more fooling the Feds and so on.

Still, nostalgia for the good-old-time good times is hardly the definitive characteristic of the childhood and family experiences he recalls with so much feeling in "Me and My Old Man." Nor can his attitude toward his father be called idolatrous. It is now very pleasant to remember some of the long highway trips they made in the truck together and baseball games and fantasies they shared. But the fact is his old man (who was a family maverick to begin with) was a hell of a problem to come to terms with. Indeed, it was not until Hemphill came back from his year at Harvard and decided to overlook his father's racial hang-ups, among other things, that he finally found his present appreciation for his father's "involvement in and passion for life, his willingness to take on the world if necessary," and his disposition to hang in there, win, lose, or draw.

Nor does Hemphill recount his misadventures as a Class D baseball novice to commemorate any days of youthful glory. They were miserable days of very thin hope and great anguish and disappointment. Furthermore, what everybody else down there in Class D was about above everything else was making it the hell out of there and into the big leagues, which was strictly up north in those days. And most would never come as close as the failed "bonus babies" dug up for "Whatever Happened to Whatsisname?" On the other hand, Bob Sufferidge, the all-time all-American from Tennessee, has had some absolutely splendid days at the very summit of national acclaim. But if he is an example of a good ole poor white boy hanging with it, Hemphill better forget it. As for such contemporary marvels as mortician Ray Ligon of the Death Hilton, Judge Roy Hofheintz of the Houston Astrodome, the Georgia "folk" movie moguls, such new-style evangelists as Oral Roberts and Mike Gilchrist, and the new best-selling hillbilly singers, and so on and on and on, are they to be more admired than puzzled over?

The Good Old Boys is not nearly so free of old-time rebel-hooping sentimentality as was Marshall Frady's *Wallace* of several years ago. Nevertheless, as a result of treating poor white Southerners as colorful, and even legendary—but still flesh-and-blood human beings—Hemphill gets much closer to the actual texture of circumstances in the South today than do the so-called findings of survey technicians, the validity, reliability, and comprehensiveness of whose methodology is supposed to go without saying, but whose obligatory social relevance somehow always seems to lead them to downgrade intrinsic human values and potentialities in favor of welfare statistics. Anyway, anybody who thinks you have to be well-to-do and politically powerful *before* you can be colorful or fabulous not only knows nothing at all of Southerners but very little about human nature.

But perhaps best of all, Paul Hemphill himself (who sometimes thinks of himself as a failed baseball player but is clearly a big-league journalist, and is also the true hero of *The Good Old Boys*) may just turn out to be one of a new breed of pretty good old boys who in the end are likely to be of far more worth to the best interests of the nation at large than any except a few of those from the good old days. Already—or so his sober ambivalence toward his father seems to indicate—he is one who is beyond embracing, or in any case defending, all of the worst shortcomings of the South because he prefers to live there. It's almost enough to raise your outrage tolerance level for square dancing and Grand Ole Opry music.

| The "Reconstruction" of
Robert Penn Warren

Robert Penn Warren, a white Anglo-Saxon Protestant Southerner, a onetime apologist for segregation, a longtime colleague of the old agrarian romantics, and a sometime friend of countless white supremacists and even Dixiecrats, has written a new book which is perhaps the very best inside report on the Negro civil rights movement by anyone so far. In spite of several ridiculous flaws, which are much more characteristic of certain New York indoor intellectuals than of a worldly, realistic, and thoughtful son of a hardheaded old Kentucky dirt farmer, *Who Speaks for the Negro?* deserves the widest possible circulation.

The title is misleading. This is not only a book about current U.S. Negro leaders and spokesmen. It is really a book about the fundamentals of citizenship which the author, a top-flight novelist, poet, and critic, compiled from a series of taped interviews and interspersed with his own reactions and commentary. It is also by far the most comprehensive treatment of the complex issues in the civil rights controversy on record. For the most part it is also the most objective. But even when it is most personal its accuracy is seldom compromised. Indeed it achieves its greatest reliability through the very frankness with which it indulges in introspection.

It is as if Jack Burden, the self-searching southern reporter/press agent, the narrator of *All the King's Men*, Warren's prize-winning novel of some fourteen years ago, had finally gone back into the newspaper business. At the end of the sequence of sordid and sanguinary events which climaxed that hard-boiled story about power politics in a southern state, Burden holed up in one of those beautiful but haunted antebellum mansions finishing a book about one of his Confederate ancestors. He had always had a very special personal urge to come to terms with the past. In fact, the book he was working on had actually started out as a dissertation for a Ph.D. in *history*. But even as he wrote he knew very well that soon now he would *"go out of the house and go into the convulsion of the world, out of history into history and the awful responsibility of time."*

It was inevitable that this responsibility, awful or magnificent, would require a truly serious and sensitive Southerner to confront the all too obvious fact that Negroes are a major force which determines much if not most of the convulsion in his immediate region of the world. Most Southerners, sensitive or not, come to realize this in some way or other soon or later. Too many other Americans never do. In the special case of Jack Burden, his very sense of history would eventually lead him to realize that his destiny has always been inextricably entangled with that of the Negroes all around him.

At any rate, in *Who Speaks for the Negro?* Robert Penn

Warren himself turns out to be just the sort of all-American star reporter/commentator one had hoped his training and experience had prepared Jack Burden to become. As a matter of fact, few present-day newsmen can touch him. The writing is much more than first-rate journalism. At its best it has many of the finest qualities of good fiction: strong narrative progression, carefully observed and rendered detail, roundness and mystery of character, a mature awareness of the enigmatic complexity of human motives, and a fine sense of the texture of human life itself.

Warren is always at his best when he works within the framework of the novelist. He is least reliable when he allows himself to be sucked in by the all too neat theories of this or that social science. Then he sounds like a reading room intellectual. He wastes entirely too much time, for instance, fumbling around with Stanley M. Elkins's classroom theories about Samboism (*sic!*). When he sits listening to Charles Evers telling about the heroic past between himself and his martyred brother Medgar, the novelist in him spots the almost too pat rhetorical dynamics even as he accepts the truth of what is being said. Not so, however, when some postulating head-shrinker wraps *his* rhetoric about Sambo archetypes in the jargon of psychiatry. He also lets the cocktail party theorists fake him into making glib speculations which would reduce music, dance, sports, and even robust sexuality into questionable assets. Do these writers ever wonder how they sound to Negroes? Negroes think all of these things are wonderful. They are not the least bit interested in giving them up. They want to add other things to them.

A most remarkable quality of Warren the interviewer, on the other hand, is his unique lack of condescension. Unlike most U.S. newsmen, he accepts his people for what they are, tries to understand them, records their opinions as faithfully as possible whether he agrees with them or not, never presumes, never attempts to browbeat. Thus his subjects come through as highly significant human beings engaged in a very serious controversy, and his book is a highly dependable source of firsthand historical highlights of this domestic crisis over the last ten years.

The Negro leaders and spokesmen Warren visited on his zigzag trips to most of the key locations directly involved in the civil rights struggle represent all of the organizations and all the walks of U.S. Negro life. They themselves range from folk types to intellectuals. All are dedicated. All have a great awareness of the moral issues involved, and the overwhelming majority have a responsible and realistic sense of their own power. Those who have been physically brutalized, jailed, terrorized remain even more steadfast. Not only are most of them very articulate, many have held their own in the highest councils of the nation, and Warren respects their achievements, their courage, and their intelligence.

There is, however, far too much academic pretentiousness among them. Almost everybody takes the stance of a social scientist of some kind, as if one's own sense of life is not valid unless it conforms to the going terminology. This sometimes causes some to talk a lot of pedantic nonsense which their very existence and their very actions belie. None, for example, seem more cocksure than those who insist that they have been oppressed and degraded to the point of self-hatred. None are more racist and Afronationalist than those who complain loudest about being *forced* into a *ghetto*!

There are significant statements of policy and outlook by Martin Luther King Jr., Adam Clayton Powell, Roy Wilkins of the NAACP, Whitney Young of the Urban

League, James Farmer of CORE, James Foreman of SNCC, Robert Moses and Aaron Henry of the Mississippi Freedom Democrats, and the late Malxolm X, among others. There are also the theories of Bayard Rustin, the organizer, and Kenneth Clark, the child psychologist and self-styled ghetto expert, and there are the polemics of best-selling civil rights author James Baldwin, whom Warren calls "the voice himself."

Richest in intellectual resonance are Warren's exchanges with Ralph Ellison, whose *Shadow and Act* speaks not only for Negroes but for the United States and for contemporary man. Ellison is as solidly grounded in social science as most specialists who work at it full time. But first-rate novelist and man of letters that he is, his insights always extend beyond the standard assumptions. Thus he discusses integration, for instance, but in terms of the basic pluralism of U.S. life. And when he examines the actual nature of the experience of Negroes during slavery and under oppression he is always aware of the Negro's own conception of himself. This enables him to reveal the background to that power of character, that courage and tenacity, that sense of timing, and that discipline before provocation and violence which sustains the flesh-and-blood heroism one witnesses in the movement in confrontation after confrontation.

Robert Penn Warren, still the professional Southerner in spite of himself, sitting in his New England study with his fresh travel memories, notes and tape recorder, and the voices of Yankees outside his window, has gone a long way from Pondy Woods and such smug provincialisms as "Nigger, your breed ain't metaphysical." He had gone a great distance when he wrote *Segregation,* his account of the inner conflict in the South in 1956; and was a bit farther on when he wrote *The Legacy of the Civil War.*

Like most Americans, he still has a long way to go. But like an increasing number of Southerners, among them Lyndon B. Johnson of Texas and Ralph McGill of Georgia, he is much farther along than many damn Yankees, including some black ones, who thought they were there already.

SIX | Louis Armstrong in His
Own Words

There came a time when Louis Armstrong decided that his importance as a musician and his status as a worldwide American entertainer and "ambassador of goodwill" were such that he should produce his own personal documentation of his career. The first of those efforts was published in 1936, when Armstrong himself was not yet thirty-six years old. Its title was *Swing That Music.* No collaborator, editor, or ghostwriter was identified, not even when the book was reissued fifty-seven years later. Most of the personal information may well have come directly from Armstrong or was presumably approved by him, but not even the inscription in the book comes across as a credible approximation of either his voice on the page or his point of view. It runs as follows: *"To the memory of the Original 'Dixieland Five,' to 'King' Oliver, to 'Bix' Beiderbecke and Eddie Lang, now gone, and those other pioneers of a quarter of a century past, known and unknown, who created and carried to the world a native American music, who created swing. And, finally, to the young musicians of today who will carry it on.*"

The grateful list of specific names is not intended to be comprehensive, of course; but given the restricted nature of social relations in New Orleans when he was growing up there, did Armstrong himself really think of the Original Dixieland Five as being more crucial to his conception of music than the legend of Buddy Bolden, who came before King Oliver? And what about Mr. Peter Davis, who as bandmaster at the Waifs' Home turned him into a cornet player in the first place? And what about the definitive influence of the blues and of ragtime piano players including Tony Jackson and also of old Jelly Roll Morton, whose "King Porter Stomp" dates back to 1903? And what about the impact of Armstrong's parade and funeral cortege "second-line" apprenticeship upon his art, or his Mississippi riverboat experience as a member of Fate Marable's crackshot band on the *Dixie Belle,* which took him all the way up north for the first time.

Swing That Music covers the chronology of Armstrong's career up to 1936, and it includes just about all of the highlights and significant transitions up to that point, except his trouble with Chicago and New York gangster owners of nightclubs and with his manager Johnny Collins in England. But the book reads more like it was written for him than by him or even with him, except for occasional interviews and consultations. It is hard to imagine him at one of those C-SPAN book events fielding questions about the career of the Original Dixieland Band. It is impossible to imagine him as the author of this representative passage: "They [Sidney Bechet, soprano sax, and Ed Akins, trombone] actually got to London ahead of the Dixieland, which arrived about the end of 1917, and those boys took old London by storm. Nobody there had ever heard anything like it. Later on Bachet [*sic*] toured the Continent with Jim Europe's band."

Armstrong's second book-length autobiographical publication, *Satchmo: My Life in New Orleans,* appeared in 1954. It comes across as an "as told to" memoir, though once again no collaborator is listed. It obviously went through many revisings and polishings, but it comes closer to representing Armstrong's voice in its language as well as its recollections and perceptions and attitudes. Of course, the accurate representation of one's voice on the page should not be confused with verbatim transcription of one's voice in person or on the stage.

As any competent student of literary composition should know, the more natural and casual a voice sounds in print, the more likely it is to have been edited time and again. It is not a matter of making a record of things, memories, opinions, and notions as they come to mind. It is a matter of composition. Effective stream-of-consciousness narration is the product of verbal precision, not just jotting things down as they come to mind or through free association. It requires as much unity, coherence, and emphasis as any other form of effective communication. As Count Basie made a point of telling his "as told to" collaborator at the outset of the recorded interviews that were to be used as the raw-material basis for *Good Morning Blues,* the most likely effect that the publication of the literal transcriptions would create was the impression that he didn't know what he was talking about, that he was fumbling around because he didn't have himself together yet.

If it is properly done, the "as told to" autobiography represents how the subject *wants* his story told. To achieve this end, he enlists a competent and empathetic craftsman to make him sound like he thinks his voice should come across on the page. Unless he is completely illiterate he realizes that producing a book is a matter of *writing*, not just talking and gesturing. You may imagine that the reader can hear your voice and see the gestures and the action as you remember them, *but he can do so only if it is all effectively rendered by the words as written.*

Satchmo takes the Armstrong story only up to his arrival in Chicago in 1923 to join King Oliver's band, then playing at the Lincoln Gardens at Thirty-first Street and Cottage Grove Avenue. A sequel to *Satchmo,* much of which is said to have been a part of the original manuscript, but which is also said to have been suppressed by Joe Glaser, Armstrong's longtime manager, because it included numerous references to Armstrong's passion for marijuana, and his numerous questionable friends, and his troubles with unsavory or even criminal producers as well as law enforcement agencies that Glaser felt would be extremely damaging to Armstrong's universally popular public image. After all, by 1950 he had come to be regarded as a worldwide American "ambassador of goodwill," a bona fide national treasure.

Still, Armstrong is said to have continued to work on the manuscript for years; but no book-length drafts of it have turned up, in spite of claims by friends that he read parts of it to them from time to time. Now a new miscellany of selected writings has appeared, as *Louis Armstrong: In His Own Words.* It includes a 28-page selection labeled "The Armstrong Story," dated 1954, which recounts the years in Chicago from his arrival through 1924 and includes his marriage to his second wife, Lil Hardin, a piano player, who also had become a member of King Oliver's band. There is also a short biographical summary labeled "The Goffin Notebooks," which was prepared sometime around 1944 for Robert Goffin, the Belgian jazz critic and historian who was writing *Horn of Plenty,* the first biography of Armstrong.

These notes begin with entries about his life in New Orleans in 1918, and they include anecdotes about his first years in Chicago; his time in New York with the Fletcher Henderson Orchestra; his return to Chicago and stints with his wife Lil's band, with Erskine Tate's Vendome Orchestra, Carroll Dickerson's Orchestra; his affair with Alpha Smith (she was to become his third wife); his return to New York, where he played at Connie's Inn and in Connie's *Hot Chocolates* musical on Broadway; and his trip out to California and Frank Sebastian's Cotton Club in Culver City. The text concludes with Armstrong's return to Chicago in 1931 and his troubles with gangster club owners about bookings:

> Then this 'Guy said—"I am 'Frankie Foster." At 'first—I 'still didn't 'pay it any 'Attention—to 'that extent. 'Anyway—*Then* it 'dawned on me what he said—And I 'turned in 'Cold 'Sweats as I 'Back 'Cap'd—'Mugg'd—And took a 'double look'—As I said to him—"What you say your 'name wuz?: By this time he had his Big 'Pistol—Pulling it out—As he said—"My name is 'Frankie Foster." And he said he was sent over to my place (Show Boat) to see that I 'Catch the first train out to 'New York. I 'still try to make it appear that he ain't 'Frightening me.' I said—"New York? 'Why—that's 'News to me. Mr. Collins didn't tell me anything about it.'" Frankie Foster (a bad "sommitch") said, "Oh, yes'—'you're going to 'New York to work at 'Connie's Inn. And you're 'leaving 'tomorrow morning." Then He Flashed his Big Ol' Pistol and 'Aimed it 'Straight at 'me. With my 'eyes as 'big as 'Saucers and

'frightened too I said—"*Well* 'Maybe I '*AM* 'going to 'New York." "Ooh 'God." Then 'Frankie Foster said—"O.K. The 'Telephone 'Receiver is 'Down waiting for you to come and 'say you'll be there. Now—'you and 'me are going to the 'telephone booth and you'll 'talk." By this time—'Anything he 'ordered of me was 'alright—because it's no trouble at all for a 'Gangster to 'pull the 'Trigger— 'especially when they have you 'Cornered and you 'Disobey them." "Soooo" we went to the 'phone (with a gun in my side) and sure enough, someone said hello, a familiar voice too—yes sir—I know that voice if I heard it a Hundred years from now. The first words he said to me was—'When are you gonna open here?' I turned and look 'direct into Frankie Foster's face—and said 'Tomorrow AM.'

Armstrong wrote by ear. He did not write as one was taught to write in grade school, with pencil, pen, and blackboard chalk. Somehow the idea or the anecdote that he has in mind comes across, but it reads more like a very rough first draft, rougher even than a hurriedly dashed-off letter of gossip or a postcard from foreign parts. His grammar and his punctuation are hit-and-miss when they are not just eccentric.

Now, one can often get away with playing music by ear when it is not being recorded, but writing is another matter, its mistakes are not forgotten because they are still there to confuse us. The fact is that old Gates did not make that typewriter sing like his horn. He did not write as masterfully as he sang or as he spoke, his instantly and universally infectious jive talk.

The new collection, edited by Thomas Brothers, includes also "The Satchmo Story," from early 1959, which Armstrong also labeled "The Satchmo Story, Second Edition" (by which it is possible that Armstrong really meant the Satchmo Story, volume two). Here Armstrong discusses the origins of his lifelong involvement with marijuana. He began to use the drug when he came back to Chicago from his first stay in New York. Armstrong regarded marijuana as a healthful herb that should not be classified as an illegal narcotic drug, and he continued to use it and to celebrate it, even though it got him into trouble with the authorities during a sensationally successful engagement in Culver City,

> where I was blowing like mad at the Frank Sebastian's Cotton Club—upsetting all the movie stars. . . . They would pack that great big fine place every night. . . .
>
> The first time that I smoked Marijuana (or) Gage as they so beautifully calls' it some time [he wrote] was a couple of years after I had left Fletcher Henderson's Orchestra—playing at the Roseland in New York. . . . And returned to Chicago. . . . It was actually in Chicago when I first picked up my first stick of gage. . . . And I'm telling you, I had myself a Ball. . . . The days when I first found out about gage—there weren't any law against it. . . . New York weren't 'up on it—when I first went there. . . . Of course 'I wasn't 'either at the time. . . . I probably wouldn't have paid any attention to it either. . . . But to me—I being a great observer of life, I happen to notice the white young musicians coming every night to this swell night club where I was playing—and although they had just finished their jobs, they still looked fresh neat and very contented. . . . And they would really enjoy my trumpet playing with the highest enthusiasm that any human being could do for another. . . . I just came up from the South, I was just thrilled with the closeness and warmth of these great musicians, performers, etc. . . .
>
> . . . And they would praise me, which sounded to me like they were swinging a tune. . . . Beautiful. . . . So it

wasn't any problem when I went places with them. . . .
After all this knowing each other and when they'd 'Light
up, why—during the conversation, of whom ever be sitting around the room,—and at the same time—somebody or everybody would be 'blasting like Heavenly,'—
out of a clear skies a *stick of gage* would touch the palm of
my hand—or the tip of my finger. . . .

Armstrong names no names, not even Mezz Mezzrow,
the Chicago saxophone and clarinet player who was his
main supplier for years, not only in Chicago but also in New
York, where, as Mezzrow wrote in his own as-told-to memoir *Really the Blues,* "Louis and I were running together all
the time, and we togged so sharp we got to be known as
the Esquires of Harlem." Mezzrow himself was eventually
done in by hard drugs, but his appreciation of Armstrong
was as profound as it was worshipful: *"Everyday, soon as I
woke up about 4 in the P.M., I would jump up to Louis' apartment
and most of the time catch him in the shower. That man really
enjoyed his bath and shave. I would sit there watching him handle
his razor, sliding it along with such rhythm and grace you could
feel each individual hair being cut, and I'd think it was just like
the way he fingered the valves of his horn, in fact, just like he did
everything. When he slid his fintertips over the buttons, delicate
as an embroiderer and still so masculine, the tones took wing as
though they sprang from his fingers instead of his lips. The way he
shaved put me in mind of the time Louis was blowing and I
brushed up against him by accident, and goddamn if I didn't feel
his whole body vibrating like one of those electric testing machines
in the penny arcade that tell how many volts your frame can
stand. Louis really blew with every dancing molecule in his body.
He did everything like that, graceful and easy but still full of
power and drive. He was a dynamo with a slight slouch."* About

Mezzrow and music, Armstrong once remarked that "Mezz could explain every little iota of meaning in jazz, every little beat of the drum, riff on the piano, the changes in the blues and every little phrase he thought would benefit those Austin high school lads." (The latter were among his most enthusiastic fans and emulators in Chicago in the 1920s.)

Armstrong is said to have continued to smoke marijuana while serving out his suspended sentence in California, and he never stopped, recommending it to friends and admirers and sometimes providing it to members of his band for certain sessions because he thought it would improve their performance. "First place it's a thousand times better than whisky. . . . It's an Assistant—a friend a nice cheap joke if you want to call it that. . . . Good (very good) for Asthma—Relaxes your nerves. . . . Great for cleanderness. . . . Much different than a dope fiend. . . . A dope addict, from what I noticed by watching a lot of different 'cats' whom I used to light up with but got so carried away they felt they could get a much bigger kick by jugging themselves in the ass with a needle—Heroin—Cocaine—etc.—or some other ungodly shit. . . . Which would not ever phase a man like myself, who've always had a sane mind from the day I was born. . . . "

In an article in the December 1951 issue of *Esquire,* also reprinted in Brothers's volume, Armstrong discusses certain selections from the epoch-making Hot Five and Hot Seven recording sessions in Chicago during the period of 1926–27, the recordings that announced Armstrong's preeminence as a definitive jazz innovator. In the arts, the actual avant-garde (as opposed to the theoretical one) always makes itself known by its real impact, its actual influence, rather than by declarations of intent and stirring, abstract manifestos.

When the Hot Five and Hot Seven recordings were issued, Armstrong, who never produced a manifesto in his life, became the very embodiment of the avant-garde artist. The Hot Five and Hot Seven recordings amounted to a musical revolution.

Armstrong's solos became the model for the jazz solo on all instruments; and the impact of these sessions on jazz arrangement and orchestration amounted to the beginnings of an American approach to the concerto, or showcase, for solo instruments. The Hot Five and Hot Seven combos existed only as recording studio groups; they never played for a live audience in a club, a dance hall, or a theater. Still, their output became the model for a truly indigenous American chamber music—the actual venue for American chamber music being the rent party and other parlor socials, the honky-tonk, the juke joint, the neighborhood bar and grill, the gin mill, the cocktail lounge, the small nightclub, and the like.

In an "editor's note," *Esquire* provided an appropriate introduction to Armstrong's reflections: *"Mr. Satchmo Louis Armstrong couldn't be expected to write about Jazz of the Twenties in the usual way simply because he is a very unusual personality. Herewith, recording by recording—eighteen of them—Satchmo tells his own jazz story as it really happened; the people, the places, the inspirations. As always, he says what he has to say with freshness, originality and meaning—the way he would say it on his horn."* Of course, the whole piece also reads as if it has been carefully and respectfully copyedited (perhaps from a transcription) as it should have been.

Armstrong talks about the pieces as the recordings are played for him, and his observations are not technical or academic. He does not offer musical theory; but what he says amounts to a natural history of the processes involved in the creation of these masterpieces. These sessions are not only a celebration of the improvisation that is an indispensable element of the New Orleans music that produced Armstrong; they are also an extension, an elaboration, and a refinement of it, as Armstrong goes beyond King Oliver while giving him credit for setting the standards that he is still trying to reach.

The result, again, caused a revolution in American musical taste and musical practice comparable to the effect that the innovations of Picasso and Braque had on contemporary visual art, and that the poetry of Eliot and the prose of Hemingway had on contemporary literature. In the music of the Hot Fives and Hot Sevens, the "barbaric yawp" of Whitman's energetic pioneers acquires the syncopated elegance of the blues. It is not at all far-fetched to imagine that Emerson would have discerned in the extraordinary solos of Armstrong's omni-American trumpet "melodies of the poet [that] ascend and leap and pierce into the deeps of infinite time." If only the great American Transcendentalists had heard "Potato Head Blues"! And what could announce the arrival of the genuinely American more truthfully than "West End Blues"?

In his comments about the Hot Fives and the Hot Sevens in *Esquire,* the achievement that Armstrong is most happy to acknowledge is the fact that the pieces were played well, and are still a pleasure to hear. In these remarks he is concerned not with innovation, but with authenticity. What pleases him most about the Hot Fives and Hot Sevens is that the New Orleans musicians with whom he recorded in Chicago—Kid Ory, trombone; Johnny Dodds, clarinet and alto; Johnny St. Cyr, banjo; Zutty Singleton, drums; Baby

Dodds, drums; and his wife Lil Hardin, who had worked with King Oliver's band—played together better than he had expected, and his expectations always were high.

For some reason, the present volume does not include an autobiographical sequence about Armstrong's experiences in and around Storyville, the legendary red-light district in New Orleans, that was published in November 1947 in *True* magazine. The magazine observed about this little memoir that "although his manuscript contains many minor mistakes in grammar and punctuation, we, as editors, believe it contains some of the finest writing we have ever seen." It is indeed a highly effective sequence which at its best reminds one of some of the old outrageous yarns that used to get spun and respun and challenged and sometimes topped and even transfigured during those old pre-radio and pre-TV down-home fireside, barroom, and barbershop whiskey-sipping, lie-swapping sessions. Here is a typical passage: "Two of the biggest funerals I've ever seen in New Orleans were Clerk Wade and Henry Zeno. . . . Of course Clerk was killed by one of his whores when he was standing at the bar in (25) and she came in to ask him to take her back and he shun'd her and he abused her lightly in front of the other Pimps. . . . She stood back and pulled out a shiny pistol and emptied it into his body. . . . Clerk died right there on the spot. . . . The district was very sad about it for days and days. . . . The day 'Clerk was buried—I never saw so many girls crying over one man in my whole life. . . . All the pimps turned out also all the prostitutes—colored and white. . . . Some of the Pimps were Pallbearers. . . . He was so famous until even the respectable people of the city—the churches were all sad over his death. . . . The woman who killed him pleaded guilty and told the judge she 'supported him and 'hustled for him and gave him every nickle she could rake and scrape. . . . She was Aquited. . . ."

Armstrong's reminiscences here (as elsewhere) are no less a product of this old idiomatic down-home practice—it is really a kind of aesthetic form—than are some of the poems of Langston Hughes or the fiction of Ralph Ellison. When Ellison finished *Invisible Man* in 1952, he wrote to a friend and literary colleague at Tuskegee that his editor was "having a time deciding what kind of novel it is, and I can't help him. For me it's just a big fat old Negro lie, meant to be told during cotton picking time over a water bucket full of corn [whiskey], with the dipper passing back and forth at a good fast clip so that no one, not even the narrator himself will realize how utterly preposterous the lie really is."

Such lie-swapping may best be delivered in a highly idiomatic rhetoric, including the crudest forms of dialect. In print, though, these mischievous narratives will not be enhanced by illiterate imprecision. After all, publishers hire editors to correct such rawness. Talking is one thing and writing is another, even when the subject is the same. In terms of sense and coherence, what is the average reader to make of the following?

> I was still married to 'Lil Armstrong—she was also out in California with me the whole time I was out there. Also the man she 'claimed she had him 'travel with her from New York everywhere she would go to 'Massage her 'Hips.—Keeping them from getting too 'large—'UMP— She sure must have thought I was a *Damn fool 'Sho Nuff.'* As if I didn't know her 'Hips are sure to '*Ignite*' from the 'Friction.'—Later on, I found out that this 'Guy' and 'Lil had been "Going together and 'he'd been 'Spending my 'money for years.

So while I was out at the 'Cotton Club out in 'Culver City—'Alpha came out there too. The 'Lord Must have sent her out there to me.—As 'surprised as I were, that she came—I was 'Glad to see her also. 'Alpha said she 'love me so, she happen to be thinking 'strongly 'about me in 'Chicago. And after she had finished doing her 'Show out in 'Cicero Ill., which she was a chorus girl on 'Al Capone's Night Club—'Lucky Millender was the 'Producer. 'Alpha said she was so 'Blue from 'thinking about me, and 'missed me so "terribly much," that she 'Boarded a 'Train for 'California. And before she *knew* it—she wuz in 'California she gotten 'Scared—'lost her 'nerve—and thought that I'd get 'sore with her for 'coming 'way out there. But I was so 'glad to see her again, which I hadn't for 'months and 'months. I just couldn't help but say to her—"Now that you are 'out here you might as well 'stay and I'll find you a 'room"—which I 'did. So after 'Lil and her 'sweet 'Daddy return home from 'California in my 'Car, I sent for 'Alpha to come back home in 'Chicago. Alpha's 'mother Mrs. 'Smith was still staying in that old 'Shabby Apartment at '33rd and 'Cottage Grove Avenue. So since I was back with 'Lil,' Alpha went back 'home and lived with her 'Mother.—

Alas, for all the attention that Armstrong himself called to his serious and ongoing commitment to writing his own story, and to his constant use of his typewriter and dictionary, both of which he took along with him on all of his travels, there is very little evidence in any of his published writings that he ever grasped the importance of, say, a junior high school level of competence in the fundamentals of grammar, syntax, and meaning. Surely they are just as indispensable to the writing of even the simplest narratives as the rudimentary technical elements that he spent so much time practicing and mastering in order to play his music.

Armstrong had much to say over the years about musicians he admired and imitated, but the only mention of a writer that comes to mind is a somewhat questionable reference to Mark Twain in *Swing That Music*. And there is no impressive evidence in any of Armstrong's writing to suggest that Twain's prose motivated Armstrong to master the typewriter as King Oliver and other New Orleans jazz musicians had inspired him to master the cornet and the trumpet.

If he had only realized that right there, along with all of those fly threads in *Esquire* that all of those big-city sharp cats were checking out in the 1930s, was Hemingway, and that he was swinging a lot of American prose like Armstrong himself was swinging the blues and pop song choruses, and was trying to put other writers hip to how it was done, just as King Oliver and other New Orleans musicians tried to clue him in on swinging the trumpet: "Listen," Hemingway wrote in a dialogue entitled "Monologue to the Maestro" in *Esquire,* October 1935, "when you start to write you get all the kick and the reader gets none. So you might as well use a typewriter because it's much easier and you enjoy it that much more. After you learn to write, your whole object is to convey every sensation, sight, feeling, place and emotion to the reader. To do this you have to work over what you write. If you write with a pencil, you get three different sights at it to see if the reader is getting what you want him to. First, when you read it over; then when it is typed you get another chance to improve it. That is .333, which is a damn good average for a hitter. It also keeps it fluid longer so that you can better it easier."

The irresistibly elegant good taste that is always there in Armstrong's music is just simply not very often there in his "writing." For instance, nothing that ever came out of his horn was as downright embarrassingly corny as the oft-repeated phrases, "red beans and ricely yours," "Pluto waterly yours," and "Swiss Crissly yours," with which he used to conclude his letters. In the language of music, by contrast, Armstrong was perfectly immune to banality and cliché. When he began featuring current popular songs and show tunes as a regular part of his repertory, for instance, his rendition of conventional lyrics had an influence on popular vocalists that was comparable to that which his trumpet stylizations had on most jazz instrumentalists and arranger/composers. In the introduction to the original edition of *Swing That Music,* Rudy Vallee, observed: "That Armstrong's delightful, delicious sense of distortion of lyrics has made its influence felt upon popular singers of our own day cannot be denied. Mr. Bing Crosby, the late Russ Columbo, Mildred Bailey, and many others have adopted, probably unconsciously, the style of Louis Armstrong."

The painfully obvious shortcomings of his writing take nothing away from his achievements as a musician, of course. Nor do the numerous instances of factual imprecision disqualify *In His Own Words* as a useful historical document. The excellent editorial commentaries by Thomas Brothers, the author of *Chromatic Beauty in the Late Medieval Chanson,* a great scholarly service. While this collection of miscellaneous autobiographical pieces can hardly be said to add up to a truly significant literary achievement, the evocative effect of some of its narrative lines and its anecdotes is considerable.

Indeed, Armstrong's character sketches are instantly credible, and not without literary merit:

> I'll never forget the first time Soldier boy took me out to the Club, where I first heard that band play, I almost jump out of my skin. . . . The little slick headed drummer (with his hair—gassed to kill) and he kept it slick and shiny. . . . A fly would have slipped and broke his neck immedi-

ately. . . . And that's for sure. . . . Konks were the things in those days. . . . I can remember that time when I joined Smack Henderson (Fletcher's pet name) I spent the whole day having my hair gassed—so I could make a big hit when I left Chicago to joint Fletcher Henderson's band.

Speaking of Konkilines (hairdo). As far back as I can remember,—this cute little drummer in Elkins' band and Arthur Bryson, our once great dancer—were the only two guys whom I admired the way they kept their hair looking so pretty all the times. . . . [S]o you had to be real hipped and *be sharp—feel sharp—and stay sharp.* . . . And that's just what this cute little drummer playing in Elkins band did. . . . His smile was infectious (I think—that expresses what I mean). When this little 'Cat would be drummin smiling while twirling his drumsticks he never missed—he was perfect at it. Smiling with his chops stretching from ear to ear. . . . I couldn't stand it. . . . I just let out a yell and a scream. . . . It was too much. . . . Folks—that little drummer was Lionel Hampton. . . .

Brothers's book broaches also another aspect of Armstrong's life, and a far-reaching one. It begins with a section labeled "Louis Armstrong + the Jewish Family in New Orleans, L.A., the Year of 1907." This text was written by Louis Armstrong in his bed at Beth Israel Hospital in New York on March 31, 1969. It is memoir of his experiences, at the age of seven, in 1907, with the Karnofskys in New Orleans, where Armstrong was born.

In this manuscript, Armstrong expresses his gratitude to one Dr. Gary Zucker, whose treatment pulled him twice through intensive care. The expert and tender ministrations that he received at Beth Israel put him in mind of the warm, caring relationship he had enjoyed with the Karnofsky family, for whom he worked when he was a boy. Hearing Dr. Zucker singing "Russian Lullaby," he writes: "This is the song that I sang when I was seven years old—with the

Karnofsky family when I was working with them, every night at their house when Mother Karnofsky would rock the Baby David to sleep. Then I would go home—across the track, cross town to *May-Ann* and *Mama Lucy* my mother and sister." And a few paragraphs later, he goes on to say: "I had a long time admiration for the Jewish People. Especially with their long time of courage, taking So Much Abuse for so long. I was only *Seven* years old but I could easily see all the *ungodly treatment* that the White Folks were handing the poor *Jewish* family whom I worked for. . . . Even '*my race*,' the Negroes, the way I saw it, they were having a little *better* Break than the *Jewish* people, with jobs a plenty around. Of course, we can understand all the situations and handicaps that was going on, but to me we were better off than the Jewish people. But we didn't do anything about it. We were lazy and *still are*."

And he adds that "we never did try to get together and show younger Negroes such as myself to try and even to show that he has ambitions and with just a little encouragement—I could have done something worthwhile. But *instead* we did nothing but let the young *up*starts know that they were young and simple, and that was that."

This flatly contradicts what he wrote in *Satchmo: My Life in New Orleans* about Mr. Peter Davis, the bandmaster at the Colored Waifs' Home for Boys, who made him a cornet player as well as a student bandleader. "The first day we paraded through my old neighborhood," Armstrong there recalled, "everybody was gathered on the sidewalk to see us pass. All the whores, pimps, gamblers, thieves and beggars were waiting for the band because they knew that Dipper, May-Ann's son, would be in it. But they never dreamed that I would be playing the cornet, blowing as good as I did. They ran right up to Mama, who was sleeping after a night job, so she could see me go by. Then they asked Mr. Davis if they could give me some money. He nodded his head with approval, not thinking the money would amount to very much. But he didn't know that sporting crowd. Those sports gave me so much I had to borrow the hats of several of the boys to hold it all, I took in enough to buy new instruments for everybody who played in the band." It is curious that there is no mention of the Karnofsky family during the Waifs' Home period.

Armstrong's late celebration of his relationship with the Karnofsky family is very affecting. But I must add that it is not a very unusual or surprising story about Jewish Americans and their black employees. I recall that in Mobile, Alabama, in the 1920s and 1930s, one had schoolmates whose Jewish employers encouraged them, and even insisted that they go to high school, and also continued to employ them during the summer breaks if they went on to college; and some of those benefactors were said to patronize their former employees who became doctors and dentists.

Many of Armstrong's outbursts are overly sentimental, obsequious, ill tempered, wrongheaded, and glibly misinformed. Still, not unlike the soliloquies in a play, they serve the indispensable biographical function of complicating the protagonist's character, by providing concrete evidence in his own words that this man whose charm was legendary, and whose lifelong motto was "I'm always there in the cause of happiness," also had his hang-ups.

The editor rightly does not allow this special dimension of Armstrong's complexity to go unremarked. In his introduction to the book's first section, Brothers notes that "there are references to 'over Educated fools' who condemn the 'White Folks Nigger.' To them, Armstrong sharply retorts: 'Believe it—the White Folks did *everything that's decent for me.* I wish that I can *boast* these *same* words for Niggers. I think that I have always done *great* things about *uplifting* my *race* (the Negroes, *of course*) but I *wasn't appreciated.*'" And Brothers wisely comments: "The document may be read, in part, as a commentary on the change in audience that sectionalizes Armstrong's long career: during his apprenticeship in New Orleans and during the first great peak of his career, in the 1920s in Chicago, he played almost exclusively for blacks; the last decades of his career found him playing almost exclusively for whites, while many African Americans resented the cultural role in which he seemed to thrive."

In any case how could Armstrong ever forget how obvious and enduring his influence on those education-oriented Negroes who went to high school and college in the 1930s was and still is! They not only studied and memorized his music, they also admired and emulated his personal deportment (the neatness symbolized by his clean white handkerchiefs) and the elegance of his up-to-date but unfaddish tailor-made wardrobe. They may have rated Duke Ellington's diction as classier, but Ole Louie's was the jive talk you also had to be able to lay on them if you wanted to be a hip man about town, a cat whose life was geared to swinging (and if you weren't, no use licking your chops!)

When the musicians of that generation came into prominence, the overwhelming majority of them always acknowledged their indebtedness to him. And when he clowned before predominantly "white" audiences as he never did before "black" audiences, they didn't go around ridiculing him. Some may have shaken their heads or rolled their eyes in bewilderment and exasperation—as Ralph Ellison, whose admiration of Armstrong's musical tone and inventiveness was second to none, used to say, "Man, sometimes Ole Louie shows his ass instead of his genius"—but they always referred to him, and always addressed him, as Pops. And so do their children and grandchildren.

Still, in sharp contrast to the ease with which he seemed to combine the role of musical genius and court jester or minstrel clown and refer to himself as Satchel Mouth, Satchmo, Satch, Dipper Mouth, Dipper, Dip, Mo Mouth and Gate Mouth, Armstrong did not take kindly to condescension. Not even Lucille, his fourth and (according to him) most wonderful wife, could get away with rubbing him the wrong way status-wise: "By, Sweets having that baby for me," he wrote to Joe Glaser on August 2, 1953, "gave Lucille the best ass whipping of her life. As nice + sweet + as wonderful as she is she still has a sense of *Airs* that I've never particularly cared for—Being raised around people who were, just plain human beings, and loved (at least) respect for each other. And not the Attitude that you're just a musician or low trumpet player, Smokes, Reefers, etc. That I'm more than you type, which is all *Bullsh——t*. Which Goes to show, that I Can tolerate Anything, as long as it doesn't interfere with my trumpet."

The primary emphasis in *Louis Armstrong: In His Own Words* is where it should be, on the wonderful fact that nothing was ever more important to Armstrong than blowing that horn. Certainly not the accumulation of great wealth, and not fame either, which he feared would restrict his freedom just to be himself and spend his time doing what he wanted to do, hanging out with friends wherever he happened to be, making the rounds, dropping in on neighborhood bars, nightspots, informal parties, sitting in with bands and joining jam sessions whenever he was moved, requested, or simply welcome to do so: ". . . you see; I've always been a happy go lucky type of sort of fellow in this way—I never tried in no way to ever be *real real* filthy rich like some people do and after they do they die just the same.—

"But Mary-Ann had already 'hipped to what was happening in this healthful wide beautiful world. . . . So, by me doing that (even before I heard of gage) I was always the happiest young trumpet player that anyone ever wanted to meet. . . . From this first time I picked up my trumpet, or the one that was out to the Orphanage, I was a popular youngster. . . . Success has always been—mine. . . ."

The wide range of autobiographical documentation that Brothers has included in this volume makes it a very significant source for the study of Louis Armstrong. Meanwhile, for those in search of an Armstrong memoir that transcends the obvious limitations of the most provincial dimensions of the idiomatic and yet retains the entirely convincing flavor of his voice much the same as his music does, there remains "Louis Armstrong: A Self-Portrait," the interview by Richard Meryman that was published as the cover story in the April 15, 1966, issue of *Life* magazine and was slightly expanded and republished as a small and handsome volume (with illustrations) by the Eakins Press, New York. It is still unsurpassed. Meryman used expertly crafted questions, and he repeated them shrewdly, and then shaped Armstrong's various answers into a fine, uninterrupted narrative. In the Armstrong centennial that is upon us, surely Armstrong's only successful exercise in as-told-to autobiography should be made available again.

If getting the voice on the page is the objective, consider

the Armstrong-Meryman vamp: "I'm always wondering if it would have been best in my life if I'd stayed like I was in New Orleans, having a ball. I was very much contented just to be around and play with the old timers. And the money I made—I lived off of it. I wonder if I would have enjoyed that better than all this big mucky-muck traveling all over the world—which is nice, meeting all those people, being high on the horse, all *grandioso*. All this life I have now—I didn't suggest it. I would say it was all wished on me. Over the years you find you can't stay no longer where you are, you must go on a little higher now—and that's the way it all came about. I couldn't get away from what's happened to me."

And here is the outchorus: "I've had some great ovations in my time. When people do that they must feel *something* within themselves. I mean you don't go around waking people up to the effect of saying, 'You know, this music is art.' But, it's got to be art because the world has recognized our music from New Orleans, else it would have been dead today. But I always let the other fellow talk about art. 'Cause when we was doing it, we was just glad to be working up on that stage. So for me to be still on earth to hear that word, sounds pretty good. I'm just grateful for every little iota.

"Some cats wants pats on the back, and they wants you to kneel down 'cause they did this and did that and they are so and so. But I still feel I'm just an ordinary human being trying to enjoy the work I live. It's something to know you still can make that call when the man say, 'All on.' That's enough wonderment for me. . . ."

And not for him only.

ONE | Manhattan in the Twenties

It was during the ten-year period beginning in November 1918 that New York City not only consolidated its status as undisputed culture capital of the United States, and indeed of the Western Hemisphere, but also accelerated its irrepressible momentum of urban influence and prestige that led to the unrivaled global preeminence it enjoys today.

Already long gone were the pre-world-class days of the Philadelphia and Boston of the Revolutionary War era and the Boston of what is sometimes called the period of the flowering of New England and sometimes the American Renaissance. Also preliminary to the war there had been the New York of Herman Melville and Walt Whitman, to which came Mark Twain to spend his final years. Nor was the identity and sensibility of Henry James in any of his phases ever anything other than that of a cosmopolitan or, in all events, international New Yorker, a Manhattanite abroad.

And now came the postwar decade of the Roaring Twenties, with its deluxe sedans and sporty roadsters and increasingly available flivvers and jitneys, with the newly ratified Eighteenth Amendment issuing in the Prohibition Era with its bootleg liquor and heyday of gangster-affiliated speakeasy nightspots, a time also known as that of the newly liberated post-Victorian generation of flaming youth, with its cocktail-sipping, cigarette-flourishing, bobbed-hair, and short-skirt-flaunting flappers swishing about with their ever so debonair playboy and/or sugar daddy escorts.

Such, in fact, was the seemingly undauntable exuberance of the new lifestyle that came with postwar prosperity that the decade was already being referred to as the Jazz Age as early on as 1922. Young F. Scott Fitzgerald, a novelist from the Midwest by way of Princeton, who, along with Ernest Hemingway and William Faulkner, was to become one of the most celebrated American writers of the twentieth century, published a collection of fiction entitled *Tales of the Jazz Age* that year. He had published *This Side of Paradise,* his first novel, in 1920; *Flappers and Philosophers,* another collection of stories, including "Bernice Bobs Her Hair," in 1921. *The Beautiful and Damned,* a second novel, was also published, in 1922. *The Great Gatsby,* his masterpiece, came in 1925. President Warren G. Harding referred to the postwar period as a "return to normalcy [*sic!*]"; Fitzgerald called it "the greatest, gaudiest spree in history."

Jazz, ragtime, and blues-derived syncopated music from uptown Manhattan was the new rage of smart-set revelers in speakeasies and ballrooms alike. It did not originate in Harlem, to be sure. New Orleans claims that distinction, and Chicago claims a significant role in its development and dissemination (after all, it was from Chicago that New York summoned Louis Armstrong in 1924 and again in 1929), but even so, what with the dominant role that Tin Pan Alley had come to play in the business of publishing, recording, and distributing popular music by 1910, New York was to become in effect the national center for the refinement of all American popular music and has remained the major venue of jazz ever since.

Incidentally, Tin Pan Alley was simply a part of the economic, financial, and commercial foundation for New York's 1920s boom and comprehensive cultural development that had been established as long ago as the so-called gilded age of the accumulation of the great American fortunes, the benefits from which the cultural institutions and enterprises of no other city could challenge. Its art museums, collections, galleries, and auctions, and its popular amusement and recreational facilities, already outstripped all other cities of the nation, as did its opera, philharmonic, and recital patronage. And as for drama, Broadway was not only already ahead of what other cities had to offer, it was actually the national theater district of the United States.

Along with all this there was also the largest concentration of publishers, of books and magazines, distributing the most extensive range of subject matter available anywhere in the nation. Thus, such was the cultural clout of New York by the middle of the decade that for all that has been made of the protestations and declarations of those postwar arts and letters exiles, expatriates, and refugees fleeing what they regarded as the uninspiring if not withering barrenness of America, those who became successful while abroad could hardly deny the all too obvious fact that their achievement was completely predicated on aesthetic value judgments and investments made not by Europeans but by the New York cultural establishment.

Indeed, it was as if the European arts and letters elite

didn't even realize that the expatriates were over there among them. In any case, it is quite obvious that none of the U.S. writers, painters, composers, or even architects received any attention or had any impact on the Europeans comparable to that of James Reese Europe's Hellfighters Band from uptown Manhattan's 369th Infantry during the war. Or the response that Will Marion Cook's Southern Syncopated Orchestra from uptown Manhattan received during its European tour in 1919.

Meanwhile uptown Manhattan had already had its own post-Reconstruction consciousness-raising phenomenon known as the Harlem Renaissance or New Negro movement under way since 1915. *The New Negro,* an anthology of fiction, poetry, and commentary representing its point of view was published in 1925.

At this time Paul Whiteman, a white leader of an all-white thirty-plus-piece light classic and popular music orchestra, was called "the king of jazz." But actually the most authentic jazz in midtown Manhattan was being played in the Roseland Ballroom by the orchestra of uptown musicians led by Fletcher Henderson that Louis Armstrong had come from Chicago in 1924 to join for a while.

Paul Whiteman's orchestra was a much bigger hit to be sure, and his recordings and radio broadcasts made him one of the top celebrities of the period. At the same time, however, Broadway audiences that were so enthusiastic about such Harlem-generated Broadway musicals as *Shuffle Along, Running Wild,* and *Chocolate Dandies* were becoming part of the uptown nightlife scene in ever-increasing numbers, in response to which such instantly legendary uptown spots as Connie's Inn, the Nest, and Smalls Paradise came into being. And by 1926 there was also the Savoy Ballroom, the uptown counterpart of midtown's Roseland Ballroom.

Not that midtown entertainment was short on exciting attractions. Even before the highly visible show biz support of playboy mayor Jimmy Walker, who was elected in 1924, such popular annual variety shows as the *Ziegfeld Follies* that dated back to the previous decade (when Vernon and Irene Castle were doing the cakewalk, the fox-trot, and other ballroom steps to the syncopated music of Jim Europe's prewar dance band) came into their heyday and were followed by *George White's Scandals* and *Earl Carroll's Vanities*. Then there was also the more tightly constructed musical comedy establishing itself and replacing the operetta in the process.

Still, it was uptown music and dance that was to provide the decade's most felicitous symbols. Nothing evokes the twenties of the speakeasies, roadsters, flappers, and underlying mood of *The Great Gatsby* more movingly than the shimmy, the breakdown, the black bottom, and above all the Charleston, the dance, as well as James P. Johnson's stride piano, the elegant fun of which was a joyous counteragent to the pervasive banality suggested by T. S. Eliot's *The Wasteland,* the most prestigious literary statement of the times.

Nor should it be forgotten that it was during this decade that such uptown musical devices and conventions as the twelve-bar blues chorus, the thirty-two-bar pop song chorus, the break, and syncopation, among others, had produced Jerome Kern, George Gershwin, Vincent Youmans, Harold Arlen, Vernon Duke, and Cole Porter, among others, who followed the lead of Ben Harney, Shelton Brooks, W. C. Handy, and Irving Berlin and conquered the world for American popular song.

In sports, prewar New York had had the legendary John J. McGraw, manager of the highly competitive New York Giants National League baseball team whose home park (the Polo Grounds) was up at Coogan's Bluff and whose fabulous superstar was a pitcher named Christy Mathewson. With the postwar boom came the American League New York Yankees, whose superstar was an ex-pitcher named Babe Ruth, who hit more home runs than anybody ever had, or would for years afterward, and drew such large crowds that Yankee Stadium became a national sports landmark.

The postwar boom was still very much in evidence in 1927. The Chrysler and Empire State Buildings, for years the two tallest skyscrapers in the world, were already in the works, and such was the outlook in the entertainment business, for instance, that a new, almost immediately famous nightspot called the Cotton Club opened only a few short blocks away from the Savoy Ballroom on Lenox Avenue in Harlem and soon began broadcasting the music of Duke Ellington and his orchestra via a coast-to-coast radio network, music which (like the performances of Louis Armstrong) was to make Ellington one of the two American musicians who have achieved the most spectacular international admiration in the twentieth century.

Such indeed was the worldwide status of New York City in the autumn of 1927 that when Charles Lindbergh accomplished the most sensational feat of the decade with his solo transatlantic flight, his ticker-tape-blizzard welcome parade in New York was regarded everywhere as the ultimate tribute of the contemporary world at large, nothing less than the triumphal celebrations of Imperial Rome, Napoleonic Paris, and post-Waterloo London. Incidentally, even as the lindy hop, an uptown, up-tempo dance step, continued this celebration on into and even beyond the next decade, it not only became the swing era equivalent of what the Charleston had been for the Jazz Age and thus an extremely useful and widely popular counteragent to the gloomy prospects of the Depression years, it also helped to generate as well as symbolize the energy, high morale, and ever ready improvisation that the nation needed for World War II.

The growth of New York over the last one hundred years has been such that some urbanologists now argue that it has not only established itself as a five-borough metropolis but, for many intents and purposes, has also come to function as a five-city megalopolis that includes the northeastern seaboard urban areas of Washington, Baltimore, Philadelphia, and Boston.

PART VI | CONVERSATIONS

ONE | The Blue Steel, Rawhide,
Patent Leather Implications
of Fairy Tales

At the ripe age of eighty-one, Albert Murray is at once the patri-
arch of a growing number of spirited, independent-minded intel-
lectuals and—in the on-target words of Mark Feeney's recent
Boston Globe *profile—"as close to a classic nineteenth-century*
man of letters as one might find in this country today." I very
much wanted to talk with him while I was working in New York
City recently, and I fell into a piece of luck. Murray agreed to a
meeting because he had seen an article of mine about his most
*recent books—*The Blue Devils of Nada *(1995), a work of cul-*
tural criticism, and The Seven League Boots, *the third in a*
series of autobiographical novels chronicling the life of a brown-
skinned Alabamian named Scooter—and, with a few caveats here
and there, liked what I had to say. He greeted me at the door of his
Harlem apartment looking dapper (he sported a pale green velour
sweatshirt with Lincoln Center Jazz Orchestra logo, sleeveless

pale yellow pullover poking out at the neck, and khaki trousers). A man who had graduated from Tuskegee in the late thirties, he struck me as an aging preppy—with, alas, the emphasis on aging, because a recent back operation has forced him to use a walking stick, making him more homebound than he was only a few years ago.

My plans for a stroll with Murray through the Harlem streets obviously had to be scrapped, but that turned out to be no loss: it soon became clear that Murray lived more intimately with his books and CD collection, with his bulging folders of papers and assorted scraps of a long career at the writing desk, than he did in the rhythms of his neighborhood. On his coffee table were recent books about Picasso, Cézanne, and Corot, along with Thomas Cahill's How the Irish Saved Civilization, *Simon Schama's* Landscape and Memory, *and* Thirteen Ways to Look at a Black Man, *a recent collection of profiles (one on Murray himself) by Harvard professor/celebrity Henry Louis Gates Jr.*

Recently presented with a lifetime achievement award from the National Book Critics Circle, Albert Murray is the author of three novels (the earlier Scooter novels were Train Whistle Guitar, 1974, *and* The Spyglass Tree, 1991) *and numerous works of cultural criticism, including* The Omni-Americans: New Perspectives on Black Experience and American Culture (1970) *and* South to a Very Old Place (1971), *an account of Murray's travels through the region of his birth. He is also the author of* The Hero and the Blues (1973) *and* Stomping the Blues (1976), *a study of what the blues is—and is not.*

Born in 1916 in Nokomis, Alabama, Murray grew up in Magazine Point, a slip of a townlet outside Mobile. He attended Tuskegee Institute (where Ralph Ellison was an upperclassman), graduated in 1939, and returned to teach there in 1940. A stint in the Air Force during World War II was followed, courtesy of the

G.I. Bill, with an M.A. earned at New York University, study in Paris, and eventually a return to the Air Force in 1951. Murray taught courses in geopolitics in the Air Force ROTC program at Tuskegee, served in Morocco during the revolution, and was later stationed in California and Massachusetts. He retired in 1962; that's when he moved to New York City and began his full-time literary career.

Those are, as it were, the public facts; what speaks more importantly, however, are the years he spent reading his way through the library. When he began publishing articles in magazines such as Life and the New Leader in the mid-sixties—and when the best of them were collected in The Omni-Americans— it was clear that Murray's long period of preparation had paid off. He knew as much about modern literature and modern art as any Ivy League professor. Better yet, he could apply his principles to the rhythms of jazz and to the larger patterns of American culture in ways that were as original as they were often unsettling. More conventional critics of race and identity simply didn't quite know what to make of him. They still don't.

Meanwhile Murray continues his intellectual pursuits with a gusto that belies his years and the ravages of arthritis. His gravelly voice moves easily from the erudite high to the low-down, frequently punctuated by an infectious laughter when he figures that he's scored a particularly telling point.

The following interview was conducted in Murray's spacious book-lined Harlem apartment on the fourth and the twenty-sixth of February 1997.

SANFORD PINSKER: *I'd like to begin with a question that Charlie Rose recently posed to Alfred Kazin during a "conversation" at New York's 92nd Street Y—namely, "What led you to a life of letters?" Kazin obviously didn't think much of this as an icebreaker and made his annoyance palpable when he snapped back: "I have no idea." What followed was a long, tense evening. So I realize that I'm taking something of a risk in prompting you to think about your beginnings as a literary person and the formative influences that mattered greatly at the time.*

ALBERT MURRAY: Well, as a matter of fact I do have some idea of the elements that led me to a career as an all-purpose literary intellectual. It started in my freshman year at college. I was impressed by two people: my English teacher, Morteza Drexel Sprague, and a student named John Gerald Hamilton. As I remember it, Mr. Sprague made an assignment in which we were to write a personal essay modeled on William Saroyan's "Myself upon the Earth," a section from his book *The Daring Young Man on the Flying Trapeze.* He told us to use that as a free-flowing model to see what we could do in terms of presenting ourselves in words. I don't remember what *I* did, but Hamilton did a thing called "Myself and Tyrannosaurus Rex upon the Earth." He was writing about his pipe, you see. Saroyan was writing about his typewriter and about learning to be a writer—not minding that he was living in a garret or often going hungry. But finally he had to eat, so he hocked his typewriter and splurged his money. After a while, though, he sobered up from all the eating and began to miss his typewriter. As best I can remember, it's a piece that ends, "This morning I got it back and this is what I've written." Hamilton could take off on that, but I had never experienced this kind of free-flowing prose which is personal and poetic and had a rhythm and, best of all, *sang.*

Well, I got into contact with Hamilton and found out that he was reading all sorts of things, classical as well as contemporary. He knew, for example, about Don Marquis—all this uncapitalized prose that looked like poetry—and lots of other stuff as well. Shortly afterward, Mr. Sprague gave us a reading list. And right there my courses became secondary. I got my assignments out of the way quickly so I could read the books in the library. And it turned out that Tuskegee had a very good library. All the stuff you read about in the magazines was available in the New Books section. As you walked toward the circulation desk, you could see the book jackets on the bulletin board. There was Faulkner's *Absalom, Absalom!* during my second year at college, and I'd see *These 13* and *Light in August* in the display racks, and I'd say to myself, "You've *got* to read those!"

So I started reading and then I noticed that Mr. Sprague was teaching a course in the novel for upperclassmen and that Ralph Ellison and a bunch of people were taking it. Well, I was curious about that and figured I'd better prepare to take it. And the first novel I read in college was *Tom Jones*. That continued ever since—reading classics as well as contemporary authors.

I was also terribly interested in the periodicals room—book reviews and what was happening generally. But I guess it was the literary anthologies and historical surveys that grabbed my attention the most. In fact, the first books I checked out of the library at Tuskegee were not assigned ones, but rather things like *The Golden Thread* by Philo M. Buck, *A Treasury of the Theatre* by Burns Mantle, or Sheldon Cheney's *The Theatre: Three Thousand Years of Drama, Acting and Stagecraft*. These made me cosmopolitan because they took me all the way back not only to Greek ritual and myth but also to Indian plays, Noh plays, all that. You see, I wanted to know about the literature of the world, and I began during my freshman year.

But I'm told that you were a pretty good storyteller even before you arrived at Tuskegee.

That's true. I also had a good memory. In high school I was involved with the theater and could remember my lines for act one by the time we had our first rehearsal. And when we got to act two, I knew my lines, but also everybody else's lines for act one. I continued acting in the little theater at Tuskegee, but now I had the benefit of all the reading I was doing in the history of world theater. All that's where, years after, stuff like commedia dell'arte began to dovetail with jazz.

That's what I want to get to—how the various aspects of your education contributed to your unified theory of American culture and identity.

Well, you were interested in jazz and blues as a matter of course. It was all around me. The same thing became true for Hollywood films and lots of other things. But it was putting them together that was the real trick. I suspect that my ability to understand the theater, and to know almost instinctively that the key to learning a part—and, later, to help others learn their parts—was an appreciation of the *story* being told. The same thing is probably true for the mythic stories that a culture tells, or tries to tell. Anyway, in college I began reading theater critics like Brooks Atkinson and John Mason Brown, the New York newspapers which were in the library, and lots of magazines like *Theatre Arts Monthly* and *Stage*. I read Stark Young's book on the theater. We had all of it at Tuskegee, and it did wonders for my imagination and my sense of what the world was about.

You make Tuskegee Institute sound like an exciting intellectual place.

For me, it *was*.

How, then, do you account for the fact that Ralph Ellison apparently didn't find it so exciting—at least if we rely on the portrait of his college days presented in Invisible Man?

He's a different personality. If you compare Scooter's college days with those of *Invisible Man,* you wouldn't think that they attended the same school. But you've got to remember that I wasn't concerned about the goddamn administration; I was concerned about what was in the library and what I was going to get out of this time I had in college. What positions the administration had I didn't know, and I didn't care to know. All I knew was that a teacher was going to come into the class and I wanted to be ready for him. I did not feel I was mature enough to make decisions about administrative matters. I had mostly contempt for the students who went off half-cocked in protests about some administrative ruling. I wasn't about to get kicked out of school over some protest rally. Man, I just barely got to school in the first place. I didn't have money enough to get home for Christmas, and I wasn't about to be an activist. I was there to get my education. I could just see it—because I was already a novelist in my mind—on the goddamn bus to Mobile by myself and all the people at home saying, "Albert Murray's back. They kicked him out of Tuskegee because he was up there running around with some of these other students and they're jumping the administration. What makes them think they know more about running a college than the teachers? What are they doing up there? That Murray guy can't even pay his way!" And they'd be right too. Man, I had to win scholarships every year.

Can we connect what you've just said with my sense that the phrase "protest literature" is a contradiction in terms?

I agree. Look, protest literature is a form of discourse all right, but only a genius can make it work by going beyond what it's designed to do. At its best, I suppose that protest literature could be close to the function of very important satire—in terms of dynamics. You know, spoofing something that is really out there at the time. And if you're good enough, it'll go beyond that. But it's got to go beyond *that* in order to be literature. Otherwise it's just campaign sloganeering, it seems to me. If you're interested in the human predicament and human possibilities on the earth, you're concerned with something more fundamental than a structure that might change in two, four, or six years, depending on who gets into office.

What I came to realize when I started studying Marxism was that it doesn't matter so much whatever form of government we have, it will be run by *politicians*. As for myself, I didn't even want to be president of the class. I didn't want to be president of the student body. And when I began teaching, I certainly didn't want to be the dean. I just wanted my tweed jacket, my contrasting slacks, and my books—and to be better-looking than Ronald Colman or Robert Donat.

Am I right in thinking that Ralph Ellison's mythic sense of what Tuskegee was and your own myth of college come to pretty much the same thing—namely, that all experience is finally shaped by some mythic story or other?

Absolutely. But remember that my memory of Tuskegee is mythic, too, and no less mythic than Ralph's was. What my sensibility attached itself to and gave emphasis to, and what his gave emphasis to, may have differed, but we became friends and never had any clashes about how he saw Tuskegee.

He had certain criticisms which always struck me more as matters of implication rather than documentation, and as such, I could accept the validity of his statements. But I was not concerned with those implications. I was concerned with the protagonist himself and what he could do. And I perceived no obstructions of the nature that some people think he saw.

Now, when you did the Scooter novels, how aware were you of the Bildungsroman *tradition, and perhaps even of specific books that served you as models?*

The Scooter books were definitely part of that. The Stephen from James Joyce's *A Portrait of the Artist as a Young Man,* a novel I knew well, as I knew Goethe's *Wilhelm Meister.* And certainly Thomas Mann's *Joseph.* All finally, I suppose—all heroes of all fiction. Odysseus, for example. At one point in *Seven League Boots,* we see Scooter as Ulysses, but at another point he's Telemachus. The same thing is true when Scooter is involved with Jewel Templeton. Sometimes she seems to be Athena, but at other times she's Circe. But she's the type of Circe that Ulysses came in contact with, and she tells him the way to get home.

What you've just described—namely, the way that your characters can be protean, can change shapes and identities, can be plastic, or perhaps elastic, strikes me as very similar to the rhythms of jazz.

I think so.

And what I really want to get to is the way improvisation in jazz music can become a structural foundation for prose.

Right.

Well, I'm glad you agree, but could you be more specific about how this business works?

In what way?

Well, think of the writers who have tried to reproduce jazz rhythms in their prose—Jack Kerouac, for example, in On the Road—*and why they make a botch of it. It looks much easier than it in fact is.*

If I can claim anything about my own work, it is this: I was immersed in, and influenced by, the twentieth-century literary sensibility. There's Eliot and Pound, and the fallout from Yeats. There's Kafka and Mann, and all of that. That's my context. That's my conception of what prose is. I know where Hemingway was coming from, and he pulled more of it together for me than anybody. Faulkner was playing some other stuff—doing Coleman Hawkins, don't you see. Then there was Proust and all of that. But at the same time I'm reading these guys I'm also listening to Louis and Duke and Kansas City jazz and coming to terms with that too. So it's all part of the same thing with me. It's not an artificial exercise, but an integrated one. When a sentence sounds right to me, it's probably some variation of the Kansas City 4/4, and when it has the right rhythm, it's getting close to what Hemingway and e. e. cummings did, and even to guys like Sandburg and Vachel Lindsay. In fact, I think of the whole Louis Untermeyer anthologies of modern British and American poetry when paragraphs came out sounding right. And don't let me forget to mention Auden, because nobody loves Auden more than me. Man, I'm an Auden man from way back. Couldn't write the blues, but he could write everything else.

> [*At this point Murray began reciting long passages of Auden from memory and sending me scrambling to the top of his bookshelf for other examples from "the Auden section." As I threw down volume after volume, Murray would quickly find the particular poem he had in mind and continue our impromptu afternoon poetry reading. He had first editions of Auden's books, arranged chronologically, as well as equally impressive collections of Joyce, Hemingway, Eliot, Proust, Malraux, and Mann.*]

The way it works, I pick up whatever the other guy's music is—in this case, Auden's—and then I play a tune too. To me, you can write more poetry in prose than if you restrict yourself to certain verse forms.

Does all this—the books, the poetry, the art on your walls—seem very far from the Mobile of your childhood?

Not really, because I was already dreaming my dream of the world when I was in Mobile. Ralph used to say that we were southern gentlemen, men of letters—you know, reading the best books, seeing the best art in reproductions or the originals. I mean, these other guys had some abstract bullshit that had to do with civil rights or some other kind of political context. I live in a *literary* context. I know the realities of that other stuff, but my whole thing is to process it into literary statement. So I always thought in terms of heroic action, of *conquering* the world. I was not interested in "escape," I was interested in *conquest*. That's a different thing altogether. It's just like the old Kenneth Burke distinction between frames of rejection and frames of acceptance.

I thought, "This is a rough place, I'm going to have to be a hero." Or you could say, "This is a rough place, and it shouldn't be that way—why me?" But the result of the latter position is that you spend all your time bellyaching about the fact that it's rough. So you've got to do this, and then you've got to do that. But the way I figured it, if I couldn't go to the University of Alabama, I'd go to a university in New York or someplace else. Besides, the Big Ten and the Ivy League were indeed bigger leagues. Meanwhile I knew what was happening at Sewanee, at Vanderbilt, and at the *Southern Review* being published at Louisiana State University. You see what I mean? All that was part of it.

But having said all this, do you really want to claim that growing up in the Jim Crow South had no effect on your whatsoever?

I was *beating* that. I was better than that. I wasn't their conception of me, I was *my* conception of me. And my conception of me came from the great books of the world. That's what I thought of human possibility, not what some dumb-assed white guy thought a colored guy should be doing and feeling. Do you see what I'm saying? So I was not impressed with certain things as achievements that they thought of as achievements.

There's a wonderful line in Saul Bellow's The Adventures of Augie March *where a character says about Augie: "He has opposition in him." Could the same thing be said of you—namely, that you are filled with opposition or counterstatement?*

Well, maybe. But it depends on the nature of the counterstatement. Actually, Ralph said something similar to this in his essay responding to Irving Howe—you know, when he talks abut being much wider than the narrow box of social protest that Howe wanted to put him in. I could agree with that. But I wasn't doing that consciously to make a counterstatement, but simply because the opportunity was there. And my butt was *not* being kicked on the campus at Tuskegee. I was in a castlelike situation, and I was doing what you do in a castle. Because it was all a fairy tale, and if you can't make it a fairy tale it doesn't come to anything. The blue steel, rawhide, patent leather implications of fairy tales—*that's* what my writing is about. Fables and fairy tales. If you turn that into literature or see the fairy tale beneath, no matter how rough the surface is, down underneath is the other thing. Nothing is more brutal than a fairy tale. You got the wolf, you got the trials and tribulations— you always have something brutal and threatening in a fairy tale. But you've got to translate the quotidian into metaphor. Why not metaphors of heroism?

I take it that this links up with what you said earlier about creating a mythic self.

My perception is that whatever self you create is mythical. The downtrodden, that's a myth. The heroic, that's a myth too.

In this sense, was Constance Rourke's discussion of American mythic types in her book on American humor a particularly important book for you?

Well, that came about later. I already had it when I read Mann's essay on "Freud and the Future." That was part of three lectures that he gave at the New School in 1938. The other two were on Goethe and Wagner.

> [*At this point Murray sent me to his bookshelves again, where I retrieved a copy of Mann's pamphlet "What I Believe" and*

encountered Murray's marginalia: "This was the first thing that I read by Thomas Mann. I read it in The Nation, December 10, 1938. I was then a senior at Tuskegee. It marked a definite turning point in my thinking."]

What about some of the other writers who mattered to you—Hemingway, for example?

Always. Hemingway and Mann—then you get to the others.

To change gears for just a moment, could you talk a bit about the way jazz musicians fit into the wide reading we've been talking about so far?

Well, I can only talk about my perception of it. I had all this in me for a long time—a reverence for the jazz musician as artist along with my reading of literature as a college student—but what I needed to do was get it into focus. And I had as much trouble with this as anybody else because jazz was popular and this and that, but usually not taken with much seriousness. You had to be much more sophisticated than I was to make certain distinctions. Now, people were always making these distinctions when it came to Duke, but that was more difficult when it came to Louis Armstrong. There, the mask of the entertainer kept getting in the way.

Ralph used to talk about the necessity of putting a frame around art to separate it from actuality. So you had to have this, and he thought about Louis's mask as the comedian as functioning very much as this frame. After all, art is *not* reality; it represents a stylization of reality, and that's what Louis was about. He could reach all sorts of insights with that trumpet of his—and then relieve you of that with his final "Oooooh, yeeah." Once you begin to take this seriously, you begin then to see the dynamics in different terms.

With Duke, though, what I see is a portrait of absolute elegance.

Right. But don't you see: that's a frame too.

It's usually the case that writers are more interested in what they're working on than in what they published many years ago. So if you'll permit me, what are you working on now?

Well, I just finished a lecture that I'm going to give at the Gardner museum. It's called "The Eye of the Beholder." Structurally, I play around with jazz forms. It starts with a vamp—and I tell them that it's a vamp—and then a riff on and on to the outchorus. That's the structure. There's a light irony in the fact that I'm giving this lecture in a museum that houses some of the finest masterpieces of European art, but for all that, Mrs. Gardner's place is a part of a universal "museum without walls"; and this functions to provide models of excellence for efforts on the part of Americans to process the raw elements of their culture into aesthetic statements. And that's pure Murray, out of André Malraux.

As you probably know, playwright August Wilson debated Robert Brustein at Town Hall just a few weeks ago, and one of the things he kept insisting upon was the importance of the African blood coursing through his veins. Afrocentrism retains a considerable grip on the imaginations of many blacks, and I wondered what you thought about this. They often claim, for example, that anything Western or Eurocentric must be rejected out of hand.

Well, would you want to send a guy to Africa to learn how to deal with elevators and skyscrapers? Of course not. Nor would you go over there to learn about hydraulics. You can't argue that there's such a thing as "African hydraulics." Or any other kind of hydraulics. So if you're into hydraulics, you've got to deal with people who deal with hydraulics. This is the sort of argument I sometimes use to get people to back away from an impossibly stupid provincialism.

Would you say much the same thing about many of the people connected with the Harlem Renaissance? That is, were they also rather provincial, afraid to stick their toes in the big cultural waters of modern art?

I first became acquainted with Alain Locke's *The New Negro* in the middle thirties, when I was a junior at the Mobile County Training School, the local high school. You were required to deliver an oration for the juniors' annual oratorical contest, and the Locke essay was an important influence on my speech. Indeed, much of my presentation was a paraphrase of his central arguments.

So I was very much aware of the Harlem Renaissance when I was in the eleventh grade. But when I got to Tuskegee Institute and discovered their fine library, Louis Untermeyer's anthologies wiped out all that stuff for me. Here was modern British poetry and modern American poetry at its best: Pound, Eliot, Frost, all them cats. And I thought, "This is what contemporary poetry is." The other stuff is nice in the sense that we see people trying to stylize the idiomatic particulars of any experience, but as for what I came to regard as big-league writing, this was sandlot stuff. All the way.

But even more important, these guys missed the real avant-garde in America—which was Louis Armstrong. The whole change in American aesthetics was jazz. That was the vehicle through which America has made the greatest aesthetic impact on the world at large—and these guys in the Harlem Renaissance didn't know that. Sure, they knew

Armstrong was a hit, but they plain missed the connection between jazz and aesthetics. Duke Ellington is a similar story. So, later on, when Ralph and I began talking about these cultural connections, too many black writers were still too stuck in rebellion and power to pay much attention.

What was so good about jazz, of course, was that it was universal—and that's where the real revolution in sensibility was taking place. There was King Oliver in the 1920s, and then there were the great bands of the 1930s that had a definitive impact on many people outside the tradition—including, for instance, a Jewish guy named Benny Goodman, who had no objection whatsoever to being called "the king of swing." And he's playing with all these chitlin-eatin', pork-chop-eatin' Negroes who need that stuff to play the blues—and the point is that what they're doing is bigger than all that. It's universal. It's the dynamics, I'm talking about the impact it made on the American sensibility. Which is why I get so tired of people who point out that Goodman made more money, blah, blah, blah, because that's not the issue. The issue is the universality of the music, which is nothing if not a Negro idiom.

The formula you talk about in The Hero and the Blues *is "No dragon, no hero." Has the black aesthetic movement been one of these dragons?*

I suppose, but on a deeper level the dragon is a personification of chaos, of entropy. So we're back to the symbols of an aesthetic. The guys you're talking about are antiform. Art is about form, winning form in the face of chaos. That's why I extend the blues to mean all that. But you've got to be careful here, because somebody might think I'm talking about a physical confrontation, and I'm not. That's being too literal about the "dragon" and conjures up images of the medieval romance or something like that. Because the kind of dragons I'm talking about can come in all sorts of subtle shapes. Ultimately this stuff is particles and waves, but even *that* is formal, because a particle is something you can conceive of, and a wave is something with a pattern. Whereas entropy is without a pattern . . . you see? So these various aspects of disorder, disruption, destruction—the dragon is just one symbol for that, which is why I play around with the twist on dragons and Grand Dragons.

Suppose just for argument's sake that I take a hard black separatist line on what you've been talking about, and say: "Look, Murray, all your ideas about form and chaos betray Western ideas about art."

Of course, I'm a Western man.

But what if I insist that this is inauthentic.

What makes it inauthentic?

Because you're black.

But that's racism, and the ultimate stupidity about racism is that race is not a scientific term. Race, to all people who use the term correctly, is a matter of a few easily observed physiological characteristics: the color of your skin, the texture of your hair, and the shape of a few extremities, and all that. *But there is no scientific correlation between those physical features and behavior. The only correlation comes from the conditioning of the consciousness—and that is not the same thing as race.* Consciousness and race just don't correlate. There *is* no scientific way of doing that.

So when people try to argue about the physiological

by way of genetics, I respond by pointing out that all tests must be scientific if they're going to be valid. That means that evidence is required, and not only that, but it must meet the tests of statistics: validity, reliability, and comprehensiveness. Now, if you can't put these tests on the correlation between blue eyes or thick lips or anything else physiological and behavior, then you're out of business because you're outside the realm of science.

But the kind of people you were talking about earlier, those racists on the other side of the coin, don't care about scientific validity, much less about how one operates in a Newtonian, let alone a post-Newtonian, world. They just don't care, which means that they simply express their prejudices. But so far as getting to the truth of things, those people have no idea what the function of literature is. They don't separate campaign propaganda from literary statement. The existential implications of a literary statement is something they're just not concerned about. The only dragon for them is white prejudice.

But, to me, this seems terribly limiting on them, even limiting in terms of their art.

That's right, and that's why I don't like it. That's why I counterstate it.

Meanwhile the black aesthetic movement—then and now—seems to get lots of media attention and often lavish overpraise from reviewers and critics who ought to know better.

Well, you've already referred to the general cultural dynamics. But when Ralph and I were kids and a Negro got up and tried to pull this kind of shit, white folks would laugh at him and say, "Yeah, you'll never be educated."

Nowadays it's politically incorrect to ridicule such stupidity. But I suspect many see such stupidity for what it is, even so.

But the real problem with all this is that it wipes out the greatest fact of a present epoch, which I think of as, say, being two thousand years old. And what I mean is Eurocentrism and my sense that the *real* diaspora is not the dispersal of the Jews from their Holy Land, but rather the dispersal of European information around the globe—which, by the way, the Europeans invented. There was no globe until they invented it. It was nowhere in human consciousness until circumnavigation of the globe—Columbus and all those cats—put it into European consciousness. Smart as the Japanese were or Indians or whoever were, it was the Europeans who said, "Hey, you're here [*pointing in one direction*] and we're here [*pointing in another*]; this we're going to call the Pacific Ocean and this the Atlantic. Add it all up and what we have is the globe ... you get what I'm saying? Everybody should know this before finishing high school Greenwich mean time *means* that it's Tuesday here in New York and either Monday or Wednesday in other time zones, and you can't get around that. It's a fact—or, in any case, an established convention.

What this comes to, when you boil it down, is that the world's very idea of itself is what defines this epoch. So the great diaspora is a dissemination of European insights and the synthesis of things and ideas they brought back to Europe from their travels: tea from China, corn from America, and so forth. As good as the Egyptians were two thousand years before this, they didn't make the synthesis that the Europeans did—simply because they didn't have a broad enough concept of the earth and thus of "man-kind." What I'm playing with is what Malraux meant when he talked about a "museum without walls." Now we live in terms of *all* art, do you see what I mean? All art. That's what Malraux meant when he talked about a museum without walls, but not what people in colleges mean when they talk about multiculturalism these days. That kills me.

That reminds me of Henry Louis Gates Jr.'s new Dictionary of Global Culture, *which the* New York Times *reviewed last Sunday.*

I saw that.

Well, let me tell you something that the reviewer didn't point out—namely, that you'll find 300-word entries for Richard Wright, Langston Hughes, Zora Neale Hurston, Ralph Ellison, Toni Morrison, and even Alice Walker, but not a single word about a writer you might have heard of—Saul Bellow.

But the most obvious point they miss comes out of what I'm saying. It is the nature of Eurocentrism to be inclusive. The trouble with these people is that they always jump up and down on some small point and miss the general dynamics involved. When I went to college in the middle thirties, how many great universities offered courses in Chinese or Japanese? Sure, you could always go somewhere and study Hebrew because of the vector that came in on— the Puritans, Jonathan Edwards, Cotton Mather, all that. But my point is that now you can go to a small college like Washington and Lee—where I was a guest professor a few years ago—and study Japanese. The dynamics involved with this are that these things come as they're needed, which is when this stuff starts impinging on European consciousness. So the need for what you must know is constantly being expanded—not because of morality or fair play or anything like that, but because of pragmatism. And that's the trouble: guys like Gates turn *need* into multicultural pieties and what people presumably "need" to know. It reminds me of the old story Clifton Fadiman liked to tell about the little girl who wrote a book report that went like this: "This book tells me more about mushrooms [or butterflies or penguins or something] than I need to know."

From what I read about it, Gates's dictionary is likely to tell me more than I need to know about all sorts of things. As a student of contemporary literature I don't need to know very much about Alice Walker, for example, but I think I would get caught with my pants down if I didn't know anything at all about Bellow. I don't think you can get through the forties or the fifties and sixties in American literature and not know anything about Bellow. On the other hand, we may not have missed much by not knowing about all the female black writers from the nineteenth century that Gates brought to our attention. The headnotes are all right, I guess, because anybody who does want to read the authors can go over to the Schomburg Library and look them up. My feeling, though, is that some things you just don't want to bother with. There's no real need for it.

It's like some people who get all worked up about the fact that there are so many black athletes dominating the games of football or basketball or whatever, but very few blacks in the front offices of these sports. They feel that this is terribly wrong, but I think they miss the whole point. I said, "Hey, do you think the New York Yankees came into being because there were so many great baseball players in New York City? No, it's because some businessman decided to *build* a baseball team. He invested in this thing." It's the same thing with basketball teams. Somebody had to know the economics, the business of such things, and then go do it successfully. So when people go on and on about the "conspiracy" against black athletes, they just don't understand the cultural dynamics of how things work.

Take the great department store builders, for example. Many of them started out with pushcarts, and then some of the luckier ones moved into small stores. What they all had to do, though, was learn about finance, legal protection, bookkeeping, and all the other stuff that goes with merchandising. The big department stores like I. Magnin and Saks were the result of a long evolution. And you just can't shortcut this natural history by citing injustices and shouting "conspiracy" if things don't change overnight. There was no conspiracy. How many of the great sports venues and organizations were built by white superstars?

Still, conspiracy theory has the wonderful appeal of simplicity.

Sure it does, but it doesn't hold a candle to understanding the way cultural dynamics really work. Look, we can go on about this, but here's something else I think you might be even more interested in. [*Murray holds out a one-inch sheaf of manuscript pages.*] These are the letters Ralph Ellison sent me during the period between 1950 and 1960. My agent is going to get in touch with the Ellison estate about them, and if we can come to terms, I'll edit them and write a short introduction. The letters are filled with good talk about aesthetics and national identity, and because they shed some interesting light on the making of *Invisible Man*, I think they will be a major addition to Ellison's collected work. Would you like to hear some sections?

Needless to say, I did, and I spent the rest of a long afternoon drinking single-malt Scotch while Murray flipped through the correspondence, stopping to read particular passages or whole letters he found interesting. Here is one example, from a letter Ellison, then in Rome, wrote to Murray, who was stationed in Morocco on June 2, 1957:

Human anguish is human anguish, love love; the difference between Shakespeare and lesser artists is eloquence. And when Beethoven writes it, it's still the same anguish, only expressed in a different medium by an artist of comparable eloquence.

Which reminds me that here, way late, I've discovered Louis [Armstrong] singing "Mack the Knife." Shakespeare invented Caliban, or changed himself into him. Who the hell dreamed up Louis? Some of the bop boys consider him Caliban, but if he is, he is a mask for a lyric poet who is much greater than most now writing.

I left—hours later than I had intended—high not on the Scotch but on Ellison's words and Murray's passionate intelligence.

TWO | An All-Purpose, All-American
Literary Intellectual

*This interview was conducted by Charles H. Rowell by telephone
on January 28, 1997, between Charlottesville, Virginia, and New
York City.*

ROWELL: I want to start at the very beginning: Nokomis,
Alabama. What does that little Alabama town have to do
with you now—Albert Murray, novelist, essayist, educator?
Actually, I should also include Mobile. These places and the
experiences you had there, one could argue, went into the
making of you as person and as writer.

MURRAY: Well, I was born in Nokomis, Alabama. But I
know nothing about it, because my parents moved to Mobile
shortly after I was born. The people who became my
parents—who received me from my mother—moved to
Mobile. This was during the buildup for the world war in

Europe. So this must have been about 1917 when they moved. I was born in 1916. I grew up on the outskirts of Mobile, in a place called Magazine Point, which I fictionalized as Gasoline Point. What this place has to do with my writing should be obvious in *Train Whistle Guitar*. I don't think I could explain it any better than it is depicted in the novel—except, of course, for the specific technical things about writing. But there is the consciousness about place and learning, and then there is the whole business of what to do about them in terms of creating a literary text. It's all related. And I take it with me everywhere I go—whatever I remember from there. If you look at my fiction—there are three novels so far, and I'm working on a fourth—you'll always find flashbacks to Scooter's earliest consciousness. And Scooter is a fictional representation of my consciousness. *He is not, of course, a documentary image of me; rather he is a literary device for dealing with my consciousness.*

Your Tuskegee Institute (now Tuskegee University) experience was obviously very important to your consciousness too.

Well, that's just a matter of refinement; that's just college—I mean you go to high school and then to college, a higher level of abstraction, a higher level of intellectual insight. Then, too, in college there are more facilities to deal with and broader contacts; there you deal with more of the world. That's why the second book in the series is called *The Spyglass Tree,* which means that it's an extension of the chinaberry tree in the front yard of the house in Gasoline Point. And Miss Lexine Metcalf's classroom, with its bulletin board and its maps and so forth of the world, serves to expand Scooter's consciousness beyond what he could see from his favorite place in the chinaberry tree. So when he's in college and he thinks of his room, his dormitory room, it's like a medieval castle, like a garret in Paris, or all the places where you go to look out, to learn, to expand your consciousness of the world. And it always goes back to this earlier thing. As a writer, you're trying to put together what is called a *Bildungsroman*—that is, an education story, a coming-of-age story, a story about how a person's consciousness develops. That's what it's all about, and those various contexts are extensions of the original contexts. You see what I mean. Scooter doesn't stay on the ground in Gasoline Point: he gets up in this tree and looks out over an expanse of the land; he expands his awareness of what's around him. When he goes to school, he encounters maps and globes and sand tables and other languages and geography. Scooter is very much interested in all of these, especially geography. As a writer, then, you try to find poetic images for the expansion of consciousness and the deepening and enrichment of insight. You have to have something concrete, because you deal with these big abstract questions in terms of idiomatic particulars (that is, concrete details) that you actually experience. These things, I hope, are quite obvious in my work.

Many Americans of my generation and after have looked at Tuskegee with a narrow vision—that is, we have viewed it not as what it actually is: not only as an academic center where one can receive a technical or industrial education but also as a university where one can receive a liberal arts education. I am certainly reminded of your autobiographical nonfiction prose in which you refer to your experiences as a student at Tuskegee. There you encountered extraordinary professors of literature, and there you read far into European and North American literatures. We have misread Tuskegee as an academic institution.

Well, for a long time Tuskegee was basically a normal and industrial school, basically a school designed to meet the problems of the freedmen after the Reconstruction period. Tuskegee's intention at that time was to prepare people to be American citizens, and at that time they were primarily assisted in agriculture and the trades and education—that is, elementary education and stuff like that. But as Tuskegee developed, it became such a powerful and important institution that the facilities expanded and they added a great library.

Tuskegee was not particularly interested in what I was doing. There were some teachers who had come there from a liberal arts education. But their primary emphasis was not on liberal arts; it was on education—that is, an emphasis on teaching and school administration, on the trades, on various industrial arts, and on scientific farming, stuff like that. But by the time I got there, it was a college and it also had a musical conservatory. That's why Ralph Ellison was already there when I got there. We turned out to be people who were very much interested in liberal arts. You would think that we had gone to liberal arts schools like Talladega or Fisk or Morehouse, or Howard or places like that. But it turns out that I don't know many people who went to those schools whose books are more involved with the various dimensions of literature as our books are. You see what I mean? But it was because he and I had the same type of curiosity and because Tuskegee had great facilities. Tuskegee had a wonderful library; that was the thing that was so great for us. But you didn't score any social points or any other kind of points with the students at Tuskegee by being good at literature and the arts. They were interested in money and power and general progress, like the civil rights movement people. Like most of the people I know, they were interested in owning property or having money, being successful, going into administrative jobs, and some, eventually, into politics. It seems to me that they're about the same as they were. Of course, if you became a *famous* writer or something like that, then they'd think you must be making a lot of money and that you're powerful, and they think that's important. But if you become a serious writer and you try to deal with problems which literature deals with, they don't line up behind you, as if you were their spokesman. They'd much rather go and hear a famous singer, pop or classical, or go and celebrate a famous athlete or some other icon of material success. And that's just as true of the liberal arts colleges as it is of the Big Ten-type colleges. I think of Tuskegee as being more like the Big Ten-type school without the strong liberal arts programs that Big Ten schools also have.

Were you reading texts at Tuskegee that you return to now?

I have them right here on my wall. You've seen them; you've been to my home. I bought them as soon as I could afford them. I mean I was a college boy, not just a generic Reconstruction Negro. I wanted to be a writer. I found out that I wanted to be an intellectual. I wanted to deal with the problems of the world in terms of literary images and in terms of philosophical concepts—but not in terms of running a business or holding an office or being a lawyer or something like that. Just like another who might want to become a preacher—he wants to save people's souls. In a way, a writer is closer to that than he was to being an engineer. The writer is trying to get people's heads straight, trying to get to the poetic dimensions of life, trying to make people conscious of those dimensions, and trying to make his ideas and art available to them. So if you're interested in literature, it seems to me that's what you're interested in: how people think and how they look at the world and how rich their experiences can become, how many dimensions they can see in events and in things. And if you had a good librarian like they had at Tuskegee by the time I got there, you had a great collection of books.

I was already the type of person, from the third grade on, who thought of books and bulletin boards as windows on the world. That's Scooter's relationship to Miss Lexine Metcalf, his third grade teacher, which is where geography started. That's what she meant to him. And I'm trying to make it obvious that at each stage of his development, when other people come into his consciousness, they are like Miss Lexine Metcalf; they are other dimensions and extensions of her. That should take the reader back to either Odysseus or Telemachas. Miss Lexine Metcalf becomes somebody like Athena. She's giving instructions, as if from Mount Olympus. You should be able to see these different images in various stages. That's what the contemporary literary statement should do. After all, these books that I'm writing are being composed after Proust, after Thomas Mann, after James Joyce, after André Malraux, after Ernest Hemingway, after William Faulkner, and they should reflect that. Then there is all that other stuff you read in school: naturally it's after Shakespeare, after Goethe, after Balzac, after Dumas, all these people, after Tolstoy. You're supposed to have all of that as part of your literary sensibility.

You said that at some point you knew that you wanted to be a writer, an intellectual. When did you realize that? What did that mean to you then?

Well, I guess I didn't *fully* realize it until I was well into college at some point. I had been interested in the theater and in drama, and when I got to college, I started reading books on the history of the theater. I also read anthologies of world literature which I had never seen before. When I read comprehensive anthologies of world drama, my first thought was that maybe I could write plays like this. I was first interested in acting and directing, and then I became interested in writing plays. The first creative things I wrote were little theater pieces. But I had read some stuff as a freshman that later on I realized had been sort of crucial in focusing on the type of approach to writing that I came to have. And one thing we read as freshmen was called "Myself upon the Earth," a short story, a personal memoir type of narrative by William Saroyan, and it turned out to be a part of a book called *The Daring Young Man on the Flying Trapeze.* I have that book still. When I got enough money to buy it, you know, years later, I bought it. Many of the books I have go back to that period of my life. At Tuskegee, the many magazines in the periodicals room of the library I had never seen before in my high school library, and I didn't use the big downtown Mobile library. There was a Colored Branch of the Mobile Public Library, but I didn't use it very much, except for materials for special assignments I couldn't find at the school library, because we didn't have the capacity for that kind of research. But when I got to college and saw the great periodicals room with all those magazines, I discovered the *New Republic, The Nation, North American Review, Atlantic, Harper's,* the *New York Times Book Review,* the *Herald Tribune Book Review.* Then there were a lot of newspapers from major cities all over the country; they were all there in the library at Tuskegee. It was just terrific to me. When I visited other colleges, I didn't see that they had better libraries. For example, I had the opportunity to visit Talladega College, which is a very fine liberal arts school, but I discovered that the college did not have as big a library as Tuskegee. (I always went to the libraries when I visited other colleges or universities.) Well, Tuskegee had more. There were better facilities generally and certainly a larger campus. Have you ever been to Tuskegee?

Oh, but of course. I grew up in Auburn; my father's farm is only fifteen minutes from Tuskegee. By the way, I was admitted to the undergraduate school when I graduated from high school.

Oh yes. That's right.

As you talk about your earlier background in Mobile and Tuskegee, I think of my own in Auburn, Alabama, where, before I went to college, I read many Shakespeare plays—such as Macbeth, Hamlet, Julius Caesar, *and* Twelfth Night. *Of course, I did not understand the plays as I do now. In high school we also read Charles Dickens and George Eliot and Whitman and Hawthorne and Poe and numerous other British and American writers. But I did not come to Homer and the Greek playwrights until much later.*

Well, me too. But I was reading anthologies and histories of world literature. I remember a book called *The Golden Thread* by a Stanford University professor named Philo Buck. It gave you a whole picture of world literature. There was another book which, as soon as I got some money to spare, I bought. I still have it. It was one of the very first books I bought. It is by a man named Sheldon Cheney, and is entitled *The Theatre: Three Thousand Years of Drama, Acting and Stagecraft*. It deals with the world theater. So unlike these people who were just doing classwork for a specific course they were taking, I was much more interested in trying to come to terms with all this stuff. I read that book, and I checked the other books out. You could recheck these books out because not many other people were checking them out.

And I had a buddy who was like a roommate, not an actual roommate. John Gerald Hamilton is his name. He was from Detroit. He had read so many more books than I because he had gone to a high school in Detroit where there were good facilities. So his picture of the world of literature and of world history was broad. In school, I had read H. G. Wells's history of the world, which gave me a fairly comprehensive view that had started developing back when I began studying geography back in the third grade. But at Tuskegee I saw other more advanced and more comprehensive books. I was challenged by them. I realized that they were some of the books one should read, and that the courses I took were just *elementary* steps in that direction. So in addition to doing my assignments, I read other books. And it turned out that I was more interested in reading those books than in the assignments. I would get the assignments out of the way so I could really read about the things I wanted to know about. And I would read the magazines. I was coming across magazine articles, and I was coming across theater pieces in *Stage* magazine and *Theatre Arts Monthly.* The magazines I read took me back and forth over different periods in theater history. I read discussions of plays, and I also got information on what was being performed onstage in Paris and on Broadway and in little theaters. I had a big opportunity to expand my consciousness, and I tried to make the most of it.

When did you come to read William Faulkner and André Malraux and Mark Twain?

Well, Twain: I read *Tom Sawyer* and stuff like that in high school. In college, I also got Twain in our survey courses in American literature. On the bulletin board in the main reading room of the Tuskegee library, they would put up the book jackets of current acquisitions, and they would put up worthwhile books in little racks on the circulation counter. These displays stimulated our interests in books. I especially remember seeing *These 13* by William Faulkner at the circulation desk that first term, and I turned through it. It looked good. Later I saw *Light in August* there. By the next year I saw *Absalom, Absalom!* That is, its book jacket was on display among the new books. When I read "Dry September" and "A Rose for Emily" in *These 13*, I realized that this stuff was good. Meanwhile I was reading *Esquire,* which most hip guys checked out for the latest men's fashions in those days. But Ernest Hemingway was also writing for *Esquire* in those days. And so was John Dos Passos. Then you also saw little things by F. Scott Fitzgerald in *Esquire.* Hemingway was writing *To Have and Have Not,* and some of it had been coming out serially in *Esquire.* I had read part of *Green Hills of Africa* in *Scribner's.* Anyway, the magazines and the book reviews really put you in the world of literature, where I have been living ever since. I remember Malcolm Cowley and Edmund Wilson as regular book reviewers of that time. Freda Kirchwey was reviewing at *The Nation,* and there were various people reviewing for the *New York Times* and the *Saturday Review of Literature.*

I also read the southern writers. I was reading T. S. Stribling and people like that, and a few other Alabama writers. Then one of the big things that hit when I was a freshman was *Gone with the Wind.* Meanwhile my English instructor, Mr. Sprague, who happened to be Ralph Ellison's English instructor too (but Ralph was a couple of years ahead of me), taught our sections of the freshman and sophomore English courses, the required composition and literature survey courses. In these courses, Mr. Sprague gave us a list of one hundred great books that a well-read person should know about. Mr. Sprague, who was a Hamilton College graduate, had done graduate work at Howard and Chicago. He was a big favorite right off, as you can see from reading *South to a Very Old Place*. I have accounted for all of this in the three novels, as well as in the "Tuskegee" section in *South to a Very Old Place*.

What was important to you about Ernest Hemingway?

His use of twentieth-century English appeals to me much the same as the beat and pulse of the music of Louis Armstrong and Duke Ellington. It was great; I had taste, I guess. It was great. Of course, I could see that Faulkner was doing something different, and that was a challenge too. When I learned about other contemporary writers, I realized what was special about the apparent simplicity of Hemingway's English and how this fitted in with other contemporary writers. I was reading James Joyce and Thomas Mann. So when I got to T. S. Eliot, I saw how he was related to James Joyce. I also read Ezra Pound and e. e. cummings. I was reading Louis Untermeyer's anthologies of modern American and British poetry. I was also high on cummings, Eliot, Pound, and Archibald MacLeish, and even Carl Sandburg; I was reading all of them.

It turned out that Ralph Ellison was doing something very similar to what I was doing. I didn't know any of the upperclassmen well. But I would see his name on the checkout forms in library books, and I also knew that he was taking a course on the novel. He and some other people whom I still remember were taking a course on the novel under

Mr. Sprague, who was my freshman English teacher. They were doing all English novels, and I have copies of some of them right here. So I also read *Tom Jones* when I was a freshman. That was a great book to read with all those digressions and the stuff on comedy, and then I was reading the current books. My favorite of the popular books was not *Gone with the Wind*. It was the current best-seller, but the big best-seller just before that was *Anthony Adverse,* a novel by Hervey Allen. I thought that was a terrific novel. Later on, I also realized that it was sort of like a Balzacian novel. It was a historical novel; it had to do with the slave trade and the establishment of colonies and plantations in the New World.

But while I was keeping up with what I was reading in the literary magazines and books, I was also aware of what was happening among the upperclassmen. I was also trying to figure out who at Tuskegee was the kind of college student I really wanted to be like. I looked at these upperclassmen, and I picked out Ralph Ellison. Although he was taking music, I always associated him with books. The Ralph I knew was standing with books in his arms, with novels by Samuel Richardson and Laurence Sterne, all the way up to Thomas Hardy. I have said this somewhere else: when I hear somebody say *Jude the Obscure,* I always think of Ralph because I remember when the upperclassmen were reading Hardy in Mr. Sprague's class. I was looking forward to the time I would become an upperclassman and take that course. I was also interested in athletics, in what, for example, was going on in football practice. But books won out. Not that I gave up sports.

For the first time I want to confess something to you. You have already referred to South to a Very Old Place. *My confession is this: sometimes I go to that book to remind myself of who I am as a Southerner. Will you talk about the genealogy of* South to a Very Old Place?

How do you mean?

How did that book come into being? What occasioned it? How did you come to write it?

Well, it started out as an assignment from *Harper's* magazine. It comes after *The Omni-Americans*. Then I wrote *The Hero and the Blues* because I had been pulling my thoughts together about the nature of literature—that is, what writing involves. Then I was invited to give lectures in a very important series at the University of Missouri (at Columbia), and I used half of the manuscript to create three lectures which were somewhat like the Norton Lectures at Harvard. You would get a book out of it. So I pulled this material out of the larger manuscript and wrote what in effect is my approach to a theory of American literature with the blues idiom as a frame of reference for defining heroic action.

But to get back to *South to a Very Old Place*: after working on what became *The Omni-Americans*, I got this assignment from *Harper's* magazine to participate in a series which they called "Going Home in America." Somebody was going home in the Midwest, somebody going home in the East, somebody going home in the Far West. So the editor, who is a friend named Willie Morris, decided to give me an assignment. Instead of going to Mobile, I decided to go south, with Mobile included in it, Mobile being a point of return back north. When I got to Mobile, I thought of myself as on the way back to New York, but I did go a bit farther south, to New Orleans. As the piece grew, I decided that I was not going to write a civil rights report or anything like that; I would write a book about coming to terms with yourself, with myself upon the earth, as it were, in dealing with how I came to have the outlook and the sensibility I have. So I made *South to a Very Old Place* a book about that. In certain places in the book, you get a poetry—rather than ordinary concrete details—that informs the narrator's sensibility, because it is through that sensibility that the reader discovers how the narrator feels about things that he's going through, and what he makes of it when he records it. All of these make the story. And that's how it happened. When he got to a certain place, he zoomed in, and he realized you can really make something out of that moment, other than just a journalistic report. And then I realized that I was writing a book, but at times I really forgot about the assignment, although I used the outlines of it, because I would say, "Well, I'll go south and stop in North Carolina, stop in Georgia, and then go by Tuskegee, go to Mobile, go to New Orleans, go to Greenville, Mississippi, and then stop in Memphis," and that would be a swing through the South. But it would not be the kind of book V. S. Naipaul was to write in *A Turn in the South,* which is really a report on the South; he merely went there and made a report of a trip through the South. But in *South to a Very Old Place* I tried to make a poem, a novel, a drama—a literary statement—about being a Southerner; that's what I was writing. And I am very pleased with the way it came out. I read parts of it to audiences at colleges, universities, and other places—and I give a lot of readings at various other places too. There are often requests for me to read from *South to a Very Old Place* and *Train Whistle Guitar.* But at public readings, I don't like to deal with the abstract ideas you find in *The Hero and the Blues, Stomping the Blues,* and *The Blue Devils of Nada.* By the way, once you get the whole Scooter cycle or saga of novels, it will be as if *South to a Very Old Place* is a sort of extended epilogue to whatever the last volume about Scooter is about. It is from the type of literary sensibility operating in *South to a Very Old Place* that stories in the Scooter saga come.

Scooter is still in process. Are there other volumes coming?

At least another one, I hope. So it's just a matter of what I can deal with at another stage, which is what else you can invent in order to deal with other dimensions of his sensibility. That's what that is. Volume one is *Train Whistle Guitar,* and that's like an evocation to adventure. That's what Luzana Cholly represents, the call to adventure, the call to heroic action, the call to the world at large. Then there's the preparation for Scooter in *The Spyglass Tree,* which has two parts, one being benchmarks and the other being the briarpatch. And then there is *The Seven League Boots,* in which you have an apprentice, a journeyman, and the craftsman. The title is a reference to a fairy tale about Puss in Boots. By putting on these boots he can make a stride of seven leagues; he can make longer strides. See the fairy tales of Charles Perrault, the Frenchman. These literary references are not to show off; they are functional things as in Eliot and Pound and Joyce. Well, when you see the title of the novel, *The Seven League Boots,* you think Scooter is going to run right to a castle, but when you open the book you see a quotation from Franz Kafka which says, "The castle hill was hidden, veiled in mist and darkness, nor was there a glimmer of light to show that a castle was there." It certainly does not mean that the seven league boots are going to solve all of Scooter's problems. It means that when he comes down out of the spyglass tree he has a better stride. In fact he's playing a goddamned bass fiddle, and he's playing what is equivalent to a stride. He's keeping time. He's a novice at this thing; he's only an apprentice with a part-time job. There is nothing that says that Scooter came into the world to be a bass fiddle player. But because he is a very bright young man, a very good college student, a Phi Beta Kappa sort of guy, he could certainly learn the bass fiddle, which Hortense Hightower has given him so he can listen to everything while keeping time.

Music, as well as literary texts, informs your prose fiction and nonfiction prose.

Music is style; it's form. What you're dealing with is chaos, you're dealing with nada, you're dealing with entropy, and that's what makes the blues central to my work. The blues puts a form on you and enables you to cope with entropy.

I'm talking about art, man. But what is art? Art is a means by which your experience is processed into aesthetic statement. That's true of painting, that's true of literature, it's true of music, it's true of sculpture, it's true of everything you're dealing with when you're ultimately trying to make an elegant statement. Another definition of art, of course, is this: it is the ultimate extension, elaboration, and refinement of the rituals which encapsulate the basic survival techniques of a given cultural configuration. So that if you went back to the primordial level of society and human consciousness, and you went back to hunting societies and fishing societies or something like that, and if you looked at what they do for a living (if they survived by hunting, or fishing, or finding and picking berries or whatever), you'd find that there are games and there are ceremonies. All of these, you would discover, are reenactments or forms of reenactments of their survival technology of hunting, fishing, and so forth. The ultimate extension, elaboration, and refinement of these rituals is art. So you're always dealing with something that's fundamental if you're dealing with art.

We are not talking about just ripping off something or imitating somebody else. We are talking about coming to terms with yourself, with your consciousness. That's what Scooter is about. In the very first book, he tries to name himself. He says, "My name is Jack the Rabbit because I was bred and born and brought up in the briarpatch," which means that he has to be nimble or nothing. He's got to be resilient. In other words, he's got to be a swinger. He's got to be able to improvise on the break. He's got to do all this. That's the same thing in the blues and in jazz. That's what it is. All that stuff is interrelated, and it is so obvious because this is right there. That's why societies produce people with special minds and imaginations to make other people aware of what they really live in terms of. Can't you see that is what I think my function is, my function as a writer?

There are other people who think their function as a writer is to get white people to like black people, to get desegregated, or all those important but relatively superficial things. But the sociopolitical problems of the moment are always relatively superficial to what your ultimate involvement of life is. If you reduce life to social and political problems, you will never really be as profound about the meaning of human existence as you are when you're in church. By the way, until Martin Luther King and those other civil rights leaders came along, church folks were mainly concerned with the saving of their souls. Their concerns were not material but metaphysical. I was never in a church where the preacher preached about God and white folks, or prayed to God to tell white folks to stop segregating them. That's not what those ministers preached about. They didn't act like politicians. To the artist, material matters are ultimately as superficial as they were to those old sackcloth-and-ashes prophets of yore. But that is not to say that is not important; it is important. What the preacher, who is not a politician, tries to do is tell his congregation to watch what they're doing on earth in order to get themselves ready for the afterlife. Basically that's what you do on Sunday; you try to get your soul ready for the afterlife. Serious literature or any type of art fundamentally deals with the same thing: one's basic conception of life—that is, the quality of consciousness that you live in terms of. Conventional religion is concerned with eternal salvation in the afterlife. Secular art is concerned with salvation on earth, a salvation, however, that is not primarily concerned with material matters.

In your society, in your lifestyle which is based on your survival technique, there are these things that you have to come to terms with in order to have a satisfactory existence. That's how music, painting, and other art forms, for example, come into existence in a particular idiom. In the idiom I grew up in, music played a big role. Music actually functioned to enable people to survive. It is about what is around you.

For example, there is in blues music a certain rhythmic beat that's like the old down-home train drivers, whistles, and bells which add up to locomotive onomatopoeia. So-called black people in this country came from Africa, and they had a disposition to make percussive music that was dance-oriented. But they could not continue to play African music, because their requirements were no longer African or no longer a matter of an African existence. So they didn't play African music, but they had the disposition to play the drum, but they were not playing African music. They were playing American music, what became American music. They were imitating a train, something American, not African. They weren't playing for a chief or a bunch of barefooted or sandal-clad people jumping around because the chief wanted to see somebody dance. That's not what they were doing. If they played music, they expected people to come to hear them on their own and to buy a drink or a ticket, to come in and listen and dance. That's a different thing altogether from the old rituals of their African ancestors. But the percussive nature and the sound of the music came out of the locomotive of their everyday environment.

If you want really to study the locomotive as a student of culture would study it, as an artist would study it, you would see that the image of the train—or the idea or notion of the train—was deeply embedded in the consciousness of these particular Americans. That is, if they went to church they talked and sang about "gettin' on board." When they wanted to be free, they talked about the "Underground Railroad," which made the train a political metaphor. In church, the train was a metaphysical metaphor. All these images—that's poetry. So when you hear music from a blues guitar player, what do you hear? It's a train whistle guitar—just as I said it was. So that's where the music comes from.

The music is a basic part of the ritual that enabled people to survive in whatever predicament they found themselves. We might be talking about a primordial tribe or another group of people here or there. Whatever the case, people would evolve something equivalent to what I am trying to establish in my writing as something symbolic of American behavior. Improvisation, frontier exploration, resilience—these are basic elements of American behavior. One of my favorite quotations from Constance Rourke about our objective is this: "to provide emblems for a pioneer people who require resilience as a prime trait." You can't get a better definition of swinging than that. Resilience. So art symbolizes lifestyles. Dance is an art. How do they dance? They know that there is a formalized dance, but they dance a loose, resilient, improvisational dance. That's American behavior. That's why I say there is a quintessential American music. We're talking about that group of Americans who synthesize the American experience in a way that really represents the American attitude toward experience. The frontiersman, the early settler—the spirit of that is what is in jazz. But if you can't get people to study you as literature, then they miss the point, like missing the point of *The Seven League Boots.* You don't know that there's no castle there. So then why the seven league boots? It at least increases your stride. How do you like that? [*Laughter.*] You have a better chance of getting somewhere, wherever it is. [*Laughter.*] But Scooter doesn't know where he's going yet, does he?

As you speak, I hear a merging of two separate genres—that is, the novel and the essay or nonfiction prose. In you as artist, these two meet via imperatives I hear through ritual and through music, for example. There is no separation of the sensibilities here. I see the same sensibility.

Separate genre? Come on, Charles. Do you get two separate genres in *A Portrait of the Artist as a Young Man* or in

Ulysses or *Finnegans Wake?* Do you get it in *The Magic Mountain?* Do you get it in *Joseph and His Brothers?* Do you get it in Proust? Let's not make genres where they're not. That's the kind of crap Skip Gates implied about *The Seven League Boots* in his *New Yorker* profile of me. What the hell has he been reading? Everything in *The Spyglass Tree* and in *The Seven League Boots* is justified by the character's schoolboy sensibility. It's no stiff-ass stuff like some of what your friends write, where they have a character stand up, in effect, and speechify about civil rights. That's artificial to me. Scooter and his old roommate were *schoolboys,* and they read a lot of books. Sounding bookish is as much a part of what they were as sounding hep on occasion. So that doesn't intrude on the story; that's what the story is about, isn't it? It's like what you said earlier. You said you're taken back to the south when you read *South to a Very Old Place.* The author is trying to write a poem really, and the language is trying to swing as hard as it can. But the narrator can discuss books. That is entirely consistent with me. I can't sit on the phone in this abstract interview without talking about Proust and Joyce and Mann and Hemingway. We don't separate ideas as such from other dimensions of fictional statement like that. We are talking about a *contemporary* novel. Right? You can't read a book as old as Goethe's *Faust* and say that he's discussing some deep stuff, so this is not a play. No. It is a play. That's what the play is doing. What he says is entirely consistent with the personality of the character. When Faust needs to bring something in at a given point, he does so. Well, when Scooter gets a letter from an old roommate, we know he's going to get a lecture almost like a college professor. He's as much like a college professor as a college student, because he's a genius.

What you are saying demonstrates something I remember from one of your other books, in which you say that "all statements are counterstatements."

Yes, of course. A counterstatement means that you're disagreeing with something that has already been said. So somebody's got an assumption about something, and you are counterstating—that is, an assumption or an implied assumption with which you would disagree. So what I was doing just then was counterstating an assumption which you expressed. You said, "I see the merging of two different genres." And I said, "No. No. No." I jumped right on that. You can separate them, but in fiction you can't subtract abstract ideas presented as abstract ideas. Otherwise you're going to wipe out Henry James, Balzac, Flaubert, and a host of novelists. How are you going to read *Crime and Punishment, The Possessed,* or *The Brothers Karamazov*? They are constantly explaining things. Where is the novel that doesn't do that? And besides, there are two obvious useful reasons for attributing your sources: (1) it broadens the intellectual context; and (2) it prevents people from mistaking somebody else's ideas for your own. But, alas, I must admit that I do know a lot of people who are either intimidated, threatened, or in any case challenged by references to books they have not read or heard of. I refuse to restrict my writing to their limitations. As for myself, when I hear references to books with which I'm not familiar, I look them up.

Actually, Al, I read Train Whistle Guitar *as a counterstatement about a southern boy coming of age. It sounds as if you are revising or rewriting. Rewriting the South.*

Yes. That's true. Why did I write the *Omni-Americans*? To counterstate the use of sociological concepts to provide images of human behavior, particularly brownskin American behavior. You see what I mean? You're not going to get an adequate image of black Americans that way. You can't play poker against a Negro by just reading about Negro behavior in those surveys. You can't even play football against them if you believe what you read in those surveys. And you'd never hire a Negro football player. [*Laughter.*] Would you? Especially if they play white people, because, according to these social science assessments, they would feel so inferior that the white boys run all over them. Wouldn't they? [*Laughter.*] White boys can hardly buy a job on many erstwhile white teams in many places nowadays. [*Laughter.*] When I look at college football and basketball on television now and see the University of Virginia playing the University of North Carolina, it looks like Hampton is playing Tuskegee, or like South Carolina State is playing Alabama A&M. [*Laughter.*] You can even go to a college up in the hills and you find the same thing. Another way to speak about my writing as counterstatement is to say that I'm trying to make a more adequate image that reflects the *actuality* of somebody's life. I can't come up and look at people who have so much fun just walking, who have such a sense of humor, who bring so much elegance to anything that they get involved in (regardless of the relative crudeness of their taste, their orientation is to elegance)—I cannot look at these people and say that they had downtrodden spirits.

The Hero and the Blues seems to be more than a counterstatement. It seems to be something else.

I was trying to suggest an approach, a blueprint. I was talking to a guy yesterday. Somebody from Washington was here interviewing me. (As I told you earlier, I've been having a string of interviews lately.) What I pointed out—and the point I'd like for you to get—is that a lot of people, now that they've grown up a little bit intellectually or, at least, academically, are saying admiring or concurring things about *The Omni-Americans.* You remember that Skip Gates in his *New Yorker* profile made it a big deal. To my profound and furious disappointment, however, he didn't say a damned word about *South to a Very Old Place,* a literary statement that was nominated for a National Book Award. I was trying like hell to make it a piece of literature. He didn't even mention it. So that probably means that he was more oriented to race relations and stuff like that than to the existential problems of life, of being an individual, of who you are at three o'clock in the morning. Anyway, I think *South to a Very Old Place* should be a very useful way of coming to terms with my nine books. Look at *The Omni-Americans* and look at that stuff that I disagreed with. So I counterstated it—whether it's so-called black people making it or so-called white people making it. I am never going to accept anybody's argument about Negroes having self-hatred. I'm never going up to anybody thinking I can pull something on them because they hate themselves. Would you do that? Can you imagine saying, "I'm gonna go on over and get that guy's old lady, because he ain't got no self-respect anyway. He hates himself." [*Sustained laughter.*] What you actually hear is this: "This guy is a college teacher. He's an army officer. He earns all that money, and he thinks he's better than I am. I'll kill that son of a bitch. Who does he think he is?" That's the way the Negroes I know talk and act. [*Laughter.*] You think all these guys are going to fall out because "the great genius Albert Murray is here." No! They'll turn around and ask, *"Who is he?!!! What does he think he's doing?*

Man, I remember when he was a little raggedy-butt boy and couldn't keep his nose clean. I remember when he was going over there to Mobile Country Training School." That's the way they talk. I want them in my books because they inhabit my America. Do you know that line in *South to a Very Old Place* about how you might get kicked out of a liquor store "by looking at the wine too long"? "Who the hell is he?" "He's a wino, man. Get him out of here." "Man, all this good whiskey here, and he's looking at wine."

Such a cat might be ignorant as hell, but he is not guilty of self-hatred. So my images of people like him are a counterstatement of the social science fiction image of devastation that so many brownskin spokesmen and academics seem to have been taken in by.

In *The Omni-Americans,* I tried to convince people that they were on the wrong track to identity. As for myself, I don't like being called "black American," because it so often implies *less American*. And I absolutely despise being called "African-American." I am not an African. I am an American. And I still can't believe my ears when I hear educated people calling themselves a **minority**-something, by the way, which uneducated people never do. All of my values and aspirations are geared to the assumption that freedom as defined by the American social contract is my birthright. Man, ain't nothing African about that kind of birthright. Ain't nothing Chinese or Japanese or Italian or Austrian or Iranian or Jordanian and so on either. Otherwise we wouldn't have had all those people from Europe and elsewhere migrating over here and messing up the promises of the Reconstruction. At any rate, I did what I could. I kicked these guys' butts here and there for the stupid definitions of themselves they were putting out there. And now they are doing the same thing over and over. What I was doing is writing affirmation, not protest. What I did in *The Omni-Americans* was to lay out what I thought the problem was and how it was being misdefined.

All of my other books are about what the possibilities are. For example, in *South to a Very Old Place* you have an image of what it was really like to be a southern boy growing up. Then how could a Negro in all those circumstances you've read about in sociology become an all-purpose, all-American literary intellectual? How could he have an affirmative attitude toward this or that? How could he have nice-looking clothes, a good-looking wife, and a lot of admirers? How could he have those? Let this writer assure you that it's a perfectly natural American expectation for this down-home boy. In *Train Whistle Guitar,* you see, we move from one stage of Scooter's life to another stage of his life. Some reviewers of *The Seven League Boots* complained that "Scooter never met a woman that didn't want to go to bed with him." That's not true. It's not a primary thing of Scooter's life anyway. Sex is just a part of it. In Scooter's experience as a road ban musician, sex is a very casual part if not an occupational hazard in the world of entertainment. But even so, in the overall saga, as I relate it, each sexual encounter turns out to be mostly a matter of a *rite de passage*. All of the nonfiction books are about how to write. They are not concerned about what Kenneth Clark thinks or about what Richard Wright, James Baldwin, and all those guys were dealing with. I was searching for a way to write affirmative books. Then I wrote *The Hero of the Blues*. I wanted to create affirmative images that would make people wish they could be that way. Not the victim, not the villain. I have never seen myself as a criminal. I could see myself as becoming a Robin Hood, but never a Bigger Thomas.

Then after that we get into *Train Whistle Guitar* and that sense of adventure, that sense of what I call, in the outchorus to *South to a Very Old Place,* "the adventuresomeness of the brown-skinned hometown boy in us all." Man, that's turning that stuff all the way around. Isn't it? That's what you can do as you develop literary skill—you can constantly signify on all those different levels. That's what I tried to do in *Train Whistle Guitar.* You have the issue of adventure, the sense of adventure, but these boys are not ready for adventure. So Luzana Cholly, the guy they admire as an epic hero, brings them back. Scooter realizes that he has to go through Miss Metcalf. Going through Miss Metcalf means that he has to go to college. When he gets to college, there is Hortense Hightower, who is obviously more interested in his potential than in his body and from whom he earns a bass fiddle. He knows not to make any mannish mistakes with her, just as he never got fresh with Miss Lexine Metcalf. So when he gets out there on the road with the band, he is supposed to be pretty hep. He is accused of having made one little false move at that party where the rich girl picks him up. And the guys kid him because he didn't touch her for an expensive gift. That's a little joke they're playing on him, telling him that hepcats don't shack up with horseback-riding, sailboat-sailing rich girls with hot pants just for fun.

You speak of the blues. Will you talk about how the blues impulse is played out in other arenas of American life?

Well, what a case of the blues represents is chaos, entropy, futility, depression, defeat, contention—all of that. Now, to survive you got to have an affirmative attitude toward your possibilities rather than an attitude of defeatism and lamentation. When many people outside the functional context of the blues idiom think about the blues, they want to think in such negative terms. They want to say that these are Negroes who came out of slavery and are inferior citizens, and that when they sing the blues, they're just bemoaning their sorry state in life. You know better than that. [*Laughter.*] Folks go to the juke joints to hit on something; otherwise they might just as well sing the blues in church. This they never do. All those illegitimate children come from the Dionysian dimension of the blues—that is, they come from stomping away the blues. In other words, the juke joint is a temple where this rite takes place. You start out by chasing the blues away or stomping the blues away or snapping or swinging or bopping or riffing the blues away. That's a purification ritual. Then at some point you cross that line, and it becomes a fertility ritual. There is nothing more aphrodisiac than the blues. You don't get on your knees and pray when you hear the blues. When you get on your knees and blues is playing, there is no lamentation. [*Sustained laughter.*] You're involved in a fertility ritual, even if it's a mock fertility ritual. You're still going through the motions that are part of a fertility ritual. And what could be more affirmative than a fertility ritual?

When you really look at the nature of a blues statement, you see what the whole thing involves. You discover that it is a music of affirmation; it is not a music of commiseration. It's out of that affirmation that you get all of that elegance. And on the break you get all of those elegant movements and rhythms. With the break the musicians go to town, and then later they pick up where the cadence stopped. Nobody can be exposed to that without responding affirmatively. That kind of musical statement is a basic existential affirmation. And the musicians counterstate their problems; they counterstate the depression, despair, despondency, melancholia, and so forth. Blues music is a ritualistic counterstatement. That is what all of those self-styled victims who go in for protest rhetoric do just like everybody else, and yet they go out and write or talk as if it were all just the opposite. I'm looking at what they really do instead of what they say in their pitches for welfare handouts.

It seems to me then that one of the main points of your writing has been to reveal to us Americans who we are.

Right, exactly.

That is, in your books you've been trying to explain to us who we are.

Right. Identity—that's one of the things I talk about, one of the most basic. Reread *The Seven League Boots* and you discover that this book, which began with *Train Whistle Guitar* and the question of Scooter's personal identity, is about the larger context of his American identity.

About the Author

ALBERT MURRAY was born in Nokomis, Alabama, in 1916. He was educated at Tuskegee Institute, where he later taught literature and directed the college theater. A retired major in the United States Air Force, Murray has been O'Connor Professor of Literature at Colgate University, visiting professor of literature at the University of Massachusetts, writer-in-residence at Emory University, and Paul Anthony Brick Lecturer at the University of Missouri. He is the author of many works of fiction and nonfiction, including the autobiography *South to a Very Old Place,* and the novels *Train Whistle Guitar, The Spyglass Tree,* and *The Seven League Boots.* He lives in New York City.